ALASKA
THEN & NOW
ANCHORAGE, JUNEAU & FAIRBANKS

ALASKA
THEN & NOW

ANCHORAGE, JUNEAU & FAIRBANKS

SONYA SENKOWSKY
& AMANDA COYNE

THUNDER BAY
P·R·E·S·S

San Diego, California

Thunder Bay Press
An imprint of the Advantage Publishers Group
10350 Barnes Canyon Road, San Diego, CA 92121
www.thunderbaybooks.com

Produced by Salamander Books,
an imprint of Anova Books Ltd.
10 Southcombe Street, London W14 0RA, UK

ISBN-13: 978-1-59223-799-9
ISBN-10: 1-59223-799-1

Library of Congress Cataloging-in-Publication Data

Senkowsky, Sonya.
    Alaska then & now : Anchorage, Juneau & Fairbanks / Sonya Senkowsky & Amanda Coyne.
      p. cm.
    ISBN 978-1-59223-799-9
1. Anchorage (Alaska)--History--Pictorial works. 2. Anchorage (Alaska)--Pictorial works.
3. Juneau (Alaska)--History--Pictorial works. 4. Juneau (Alaska)--Pictorial works. 5. Fairbanks
(Alaska)--History--Pictorial works. 6. Fairbanks (Alaska)--Pictorial works. I. Coyne, Amanda.
II. Title. III. Title: Alaska then and now.
    F914.A5S46 2008
    979.8--dc22
                            2007043027

1 2 3 4 5 12 11 10 09 08

Printed in China.

ACKNOWLEDGMENTS

Thank you to the following for assistance in the research of this work: Tony Hopfinger for his awesome
Anchorage captions; Chris Floyd for his patient encouragement and map mastery; the librarians at the
University of Alaska Fairbanks Elmer E. Rasmuson Library; Addison Field and the Juneau-Douglas City
Museum; Juneau's Mike Blackwell, for sharing his knowledge, his collection of Gastineau Heritage News
newsletters, and his hospitality; Don Barnes, for an enlightening street tour of Juneau's past; Gary Gillette, of
the Last Chance Mining Museum and the Gastineau Channel Historical Society; as well as Cliff Larson, Bruce
Merrell, Jim Gottstein, Matthew Reckard, Candy Waugaman, the people in the People's Republic of Ester, and
the Downtown Association of Fairbanks. Thanks also to more than a century of Alaska newspaper reporters,
whose detailed yet often uncredited accounts helped write history or supplied clues of where else to look. Some
especially valuable online resources include: Alaska's Digital Archives (http://vilda.alaska.edu), a starting point
for identifying the historical photos used in this book; and Digital Bob, part of the Bob DeArmond History
Project, which may be found at http://www.juneau.org/parkrec/museum/forms/digitalbob/bobhome.php.

We additionally acknowledge the following books, which we highly recommend to those seeking more
information about Alaska's urban past: *Buildings of Alaska*, by Alison Hoagland, Oxford University Press,
1993; *Fairbanks: A City Historical Survey*, by Janet Matheson, conducted for the City of Fairbanks, 1978;
Patterns of the Past: An Inventory of Anchorage's Heritage Resources, by Michael Carberry, prepared for the
Municipality of Anchorage, Historic Landmarks Preservation Commission, 1979; *Fairbanks: A Pictorial
History*, by Claus-M. Naske and Ludwig J. Rowinski, the Donning Company, 1981; *Fairbanks: A Gold Rush
Town That Beat the Odds*, by Dermot Cole, Epicenter Press, 1999; *Gastineau Channel Memories 1880–1959*,
and *Gastineau Channel Memories Volume II, 1880–1967*, published by the Pioneer Book Committee, 2001
and 2004; *Juneau Townsite Historic Building Survey*, prepared for the City and Borough of Juneau, with
consultants Glenda Choate and Gary H. Gillette, 1988. On the more arcane Alaska topics, we greatly
appreciated: *The First One Hundred Years: St. Nicholas Orthodox Church, 1894–1994*, by Father Michael
Oleksa, St. Nicholas Church and the Friends of St. Nicholas, 1994; *Alaska's Japanese Pioneers: Faces, Voices,
Stories, a Synopsis of Selected Oral History Transcripts*, by Ron Inouye, Carol Hoshiko, and Kazumi Heshiki,
Alaska's Japanese Pioneers Research Project, 1994; *Alaska's Salmon Hatcheries, 1891–1959*, by Patricia
Roppel, Alaska Department of Fish and Game, 1982; *History of the Marine Hatcheries of Alaska*, by William
R. Hunt, Alaska Sea Grant Program, University of Alaska, 1976.

PICTURE CREDITS

The publisher wishes to thank the following for kindly supplying the photographs that appear in this book:

"Then" photographs:
Alaska State Library: pp. 70, 74, 76, 80, 82, 84, 92, 94, 98, 100 (Winter and Pond Collection); p. 78
(Michael Z. Vinokouroff Collection); p. 96 (Skinner Foundation Collection); p. 102 (Elite Studios
Collection); p. 104 (William Norton Collection). Anchorage Museum at Rasmuson Center: pp. 8, 10,
12, 14, 16, 18, 20, 22, 24, 26, 28, 30, 32, 34, 36, 38, 40, 42, 44, 46, 48, 50, 52, 56, 58, 60, 62, 66, 72, 86,
88, 90, 134, 140. Archives and Special Collections Department, Consortium Library, University of Alaska
Anchorage: pp. 54, 64, 120. Collection of Candy Waugaman: pp. 116, 124. Library of Congress, Prints
and Photographs Division: p. 6 [LC-DIG-ppmsc-02110], p. 106 [LC-USZ62-65217], p. 142 [LC-DIG-
ppmsc-01681]. University Archives, Alaska and Polar Regions Collections, Elmer E. Rasmuson Library,
University of Alaska Fairbanks: pp. 68, 108, 110, 112, 114, 118, 122, 126, 128, 130, 132, 136, 138.

"Now" photographs:
All "Now" images were taken by Simon Clay (© Anova Image Library), except for the following:
p. 31 (Sonya Senkowsky); pp. 85, 91 (Jeff Jemison).

Anova Books is committed to respecting the intellectual property rights of others. We have therefore taken
all reasonable efforts to ensure that the reproduction of all content on these pages is done with the full
consent of copyright owners. If you are aware of any unintentional omissions, please contact the company
directly so that any necessary corrections may be made for future editions.

INTRODUCTION

Alaska is known most for its mountains and coastline, for its glaciers and wildlife, and for the air of vigor and freedom that surrounds its miles of untouched land. Even today, the moniker "the last frontier" feels well deserved. When in Alaska, it's easy to believe that you've come to the beginning of something still in process, something untamed. This feeling of a wild place still seeking form and direction permeates even Alaska's urban places. And that's not just because of the occasional moose seen ambling along a main Anchorage road or the bears living among Juneau neighborhoods or the herds of caribou that migrate past Fairbanks' doorstep.

Size is one reason. Today, even Alaska's largest cities are specks in comparison to the enormity of the state surrounding them—the largest of the United States. Encompassing 656,425 square miles, Alaska is not just two times Texas and then some—it's larger than Peru. Anchorage, Fairbanks, and Juneau serve as population hubs for three regions delineated not just by geography and history, but even by climate. Anchorage, Alaska's largest city with a population of about 280,000 in 2007, is the center of commerce and transportation. Fairbanks, more than 350 miles north of Anchorage, serves as the gateway to Alaska's interior. Its population of just over 31,000 endures long, bitter-cold winters; short, hot summers; and survives these weather vagaries with rough-and-tumble humor. Juneau, the picturesque state capital whose 30,000 residents are swamped in the summer months by tourists, is set against a breathtaking backdrop of waterfalls that cascade across the steep, forested flanks of Mount Juneau and Mount Roberts. Juneau, the most-visited city in the state, is the jewel of southeast Alaska, a rain-forest region known for logging, politics, and cruise ships.

A Russian exploration in 1741 into southeast Alaska marked the first European contact with its native people, the Aleuts. All of Alaska's original indigenous inhabitants, including the Aleuts, are thought to be descended from a group of Asians who crossed the Bering land bridge. The Russians claimed ownership of the land and the ocean, and established fur-trading settlements. Conflicts eventually turned catastrophic; violence and European diseases killed 80 percent of the Aleut population during the first two generations of Russian contact. When maintaining Alaska became too costly, the Russians sold it to the United States in 1867 for just over $7 million, a deal brokered by U.S. Secretary of State William Seward. Early critics called the sale "Seward's Folly" and "Seward's Icebox." Not yet a territory, Alaska would languish mostly ungoverned for nearly twenty years. It wasn't until gold and oil were discovered, and the state's potential as a defense outpost was realized, that today's Alaska began to form.

In 1884, when Congress finally established Alaska's first rudimentary government, it named the Tlingit/Russian fur-trading center of Sitka as its first capital. Gold had been discovered in the Juneau-Douglas area in 1880, but Juneau was still a new mining camp just barely on the map. By 1906, gold had turned the area into a center of commerce, and the capital moved. Tourists on visiting steamships soon followed the gold miners. Today, government and tourism are Juneau's lifeblood. In winter, the state legislature is in session; in summer, more than a million visitors flock to Juneau to walk and shop along its windy streets and visit the Mendenhall Glacier. While there, they have an opportunity to see some of Alaska's oldest buildings, still serving as Juneau's downtown, many of which were spared the destruction of Alaska's other urban centers. Fires spread by strong winds remain a recurring

threat. In 1937, fire destroyed most of the historic downtown of neighboring Douglas, once Alaska's largest city.

Fairbanks, a hardscrabble town in Alaska's harsh interior, was also founded by gold prospectors. But where Juneau is hilly and soggy, Fairbanks is relatively flat and arid. Where Juneau is mild, Fairbanks' temperatures range from ninety degrees above to forty below zero. Where Juneau resembles San Francisco, Fairbanks looks more like, well, Alaska, complete with tipsy log cabins, Quonset huts, and a downtown that seems to lack cohesion—as might be expected of a town founded on gold and beset by fires and flood.

Fairbanks began in 1901 when a steamboat ran aground on the Chena River. That boat carried E. T. Barnette, who had been seeking to set up a trading post further upstream. It's said that when the steamboat departed the next day, Barnette's wife began to weep because the area "did not look good to her." Soon, gold was found nearby, and Barnette established a trading post on the river, which he eventually sold to the Northern Commercial Company. Northern Commerical continually built onto the structure, which soon dominated the waterfront at the heart of downtown Fairbanks. Surrounding those structures were saloons, little stores, and houses of ill repute, most constructed in a mad rush, and all of which were repeatedly destroyed by floods and fires of the type that regularly ravage the region. A 1967 flood caused $85 million in damage and forced 12,000 evacuations, but did not drown Fairbanks' indefatigable personality. Fairbanks still carries the essence of the gold-rush city it once was: lively, ever changing, and baffling. A new generation of urban planners is trying to give the city more structure. However, those efforts are often thwarted by the populace, whose forefathers arrived on trains and steamships, ready to sacrifice comfort and aesthetics for freedom and space.

Almost ten times the size of either Juneau or Fairbanks, the municipality of Anchorage seems an amalgam of both. Depending on where your eyes rest, Anchorage might be characterized as beautiful or haphazard, relaxed or frenetic, urbane or helplessly unrefined. Another unlikely urban center, Anchorage began as an unnamed tent city formed at Ship Creek in 1914. On the promise of federal railroad construction, growth here quickly outpaced that of Knik, an established community less than forty miles north. When the railroad's route bypassed Knik, Anchorage's place in history was set; the town site—enlarged from original estimates to meet demand—was officially established in 1915.

Since then, fortune has brought Anchorage windfalls—not just from gold and oil, but also from war and disaster. It was World War II that prompted the building of the Alaska-Canada Highway and major military bases. In 1964, the strongest earthquake ever recorded in North America, measuring 9.2 on the Richter scale, devastated downtown Anchorage and led to an infusion of federal funds for modernization. Anchorage continues to be the nerve center of every Alaska boom, headquarters to oil companies, banks, shopping centers, and Alaska Native Regional corporations. Like the original town site, today's Anchorage struggles to keep up with a rapidly growing populace. The booms have brought sprawl and skyscrapers, strip malls and traffic jams. Downtown is currently in the midst of another building boom, but as in Fairbanks and Juneau, history remains at its heart, thanks to preservationists who have repeatedly stepped in to ensure that growth will not leave this city's architectural history on the skids.

The anticipation of a new railroad brought residents to town before there even was an Anchorage town site. After railroad surveyors from the Alaska Engineering Commission began to prepare an area north of Ship Creek for its headquarters, scores of enterprising squatters soon followed, seeking business opportunities. By 1915, when President Woodrow Wilson finally announced that a western railroad line would begin here, several thousand people were living in this "tent city"—from builders eager to work on the railroad to shopkeepers, boatbuilders, sign makers, and others who sought whatever opportunities arose. Wood-frame businesses on skids, ready to move anytime, formed the temporary town's main street. The 240 acres of land cleared for the permanent town site was divided into lots and auctioned in 1915. First known as Ship Creek, the town's name was changed by the post office to Anchorage in 1915. Though residents later voted to call the town Alaska City, it was Anchorage that stuck. By 1917, the town boasted a population of about 4,000.

For much of the twentieth century, the original Ship Creek tent city site has blended into an industrial background behind Anchorage's burgeoning skyline. In the 1990s, the shores alongside Ship Creek underwent a tourist-friendly transformation as entrepreneurs built services for visitors, including a hotel, gift shops, and the Bridge restaurant (shown here), which spans Ship Creek. Between the restaurant and the Chugach Mountains to the east is the A Street Bridge, which provides access between today's downtown and port services as well as the community of Government Hill, located on the plateau overlooking the former tent city site. This portion of Ship Creek, downstream of the dam at the Chugach Power Plant, sees several major salmon runs each year. From May through October, visitors can watch urban fishermen ply their trade along the creek for king, silver, and pink salmon.

This site, at 411 First Avenue, has been a railroad headquarters since shortly after the creation of the Alaskan Engineering Commission in 1914 by President Woodrow Wilson, for the task of laying a railroad from Seward to Fairbanks. The building pictured, a cast-concrete building completed in 1943, is the Alaska Railroad's Anchorage Depot, built on the site as part of federally funded wartime improvements that also included the building of two rail tunnels through the Chugach Mountains to Whittier. A privately owned railroad had existed from 1904 to 1914, but the Alaska Railroad grew successful only after it became a federal enterprise.

Two-story wings were added at either end in 1948, and the Alaska Railroad Anchorage Historic Depot continues to serve rail passengers today. The state purchased the railroad from the federal government in 1985. Rail travel remains critically important to Alaska, though much of today's emphasis is on sightseeing rather than military strategy. Passengers traveling in double-decker dome cars enjoy a first-class view of sights from Anchorage to Seward, Whittier, or Denali, which now has a passenger depot serving visitors at Denali National Park and Reserve.

The railroad stimulates about 3,000 jobs and $150 million in payroll throughout Alaska, with routes that cover more than 600 miles and connect more than 70 percent of the state's population. The 1907 locomotive in front of the station is a stand-in for the real Alaska Railroad No. 1, which was taken out of service and scrapped in 1927. In 1993, many Alaska Railroad employees moved into a new $6 million administrative headquarters—the redbrick building visible behind the depot. As of 2007, a new $60 million passenger transportation center is also in the works.

The home of Anchorage's first mayor, this two-story wood-frame bungalow was built in 1917 for the family of Leopold David, a Jewish immigrant from Germany who moved to Seward in 1905 after service in the army brought him to Alaska. A popular local pharmacist, attorney, and community leader, David served three terms as mayor, starting in 1920. In 1924, he died of heart disease at the age of forty-three. Notice that a fire hydrant is visible on the corner, on an undeveloped dirt road with a view behind overlooking Cook Inlet.

The Leopold David House at 605 West Second Avenue is a privately owned building that has served as a law office and a bed-and-breakfast. A side ramp for accessibility and an enclosed porch are among the obvious exterior changes, but otherwise the home retains much of its original character. At the time of this photo, it was vacant and undergoing renovations. The building is appreciated by architecture buffs as an example of the conventional "bungalow style." The lamppost hung with blooming blue lobelia and yellow marigolds is part of the city's annual summertime "City of Flowers" beautification program.

The Alaska Engineering Commission (AEC) built these cottages, shown here under construction on September 30, 1916, to house railroad employees. In all, the AEC built more than thirty houses for employees who worked on railroad construction, including nineteen houses on the original Anchorage town site and the rest on a bluff overlooking the site, a community that would later become Government Hill. The buildings were named by number. The inscription identifies cottages 23 and 24, facing Christensen Road (lower left), and 25, 26, and 28 face the opposite direction, fronting Third Avenue (upper right).

Only three of the cottages shown in the 1916 photo remain, along with a fourth that is not visible in the 1916 photo. Cottage 23 is now 618 Christensen Drive (second building from left, nearly obscured by trees), and serves as an attorney's office. To the left of that home is another original AEC cottage. Cottage 22, which is not shown in the archival photograph, was originally home to AEC chairman William Edes. Since then, it has served as an attorney's office and is now an art studio. The two houses at the top right, cottages 25 and 26, now sit beside a popular downtown restaurant fronting a busy Third Avenue and serve as private offices. Cottage 27, also fronting Third Avenue, houses the Marx Bros. Café, a gourmet restaurant.

Anchorage, Alaska

The original Hotel Anchorage opened in 1916 on the northeast corner of Third Avenue and E Street. Lumberyard owner Frank Ivan Reed acquired the hotel as payment after the developer couldn't pay his bill and ran it until 1936. Early amenities included underground sled dog kennels for use by mushers. In 1936, an annex was built on the south side of the original building and was connected by a sky bridge across an alley. That annex was likely planned by the same designer who was responsible for the city hall. For many years, the hotel was a premier stopping place for dignitaries and celebrities, from Alaska painter Sydney Laurence, who kept an apartment here, to Will Rogers and Wiley Post, who stayed here two days before they died in a plane crash in Barrow.

The original building has long since been torn down, and the Hilton Anchorage stands in its place, with one tower rising twenty-two stories into the sky from the northeast corner of the block. However, a vestige of the original Anchorage Hotel still remains. Red neon lettering and a canopy on the right side of the building, facing E Street, mark the location of today's business, now called the Historic Anchorage Hotel, which is located next door in the surviving Anchorage Hotel Annex (also seen on page 37). Once allowed to fall into disrepair, the hotel was renovated in 1989 and is now listed on the National Register of Historic Places. The kennels are gone and more conventional, modern amenities, such as wireless Internet, are offered to guests. As in the 1930s, the annex houses retail space, but today caters mostly to tourists.

Like many early Anchorage buildings, Anchorage's first school was built by the Alaska Engineering Commission (AEC). After realizing that no provisions had been made for funding a school from tax assessments or other sources, the AEC built the first Anchorage school in 1915 on the portion of the town site designated as the School Reserve, a block bounded by Fifth and Sixth avenues and F and G streets. The school served less than a hundred students in its first year. However, a rapidly expanding student body soon outgrew the school, which had unheated outdoor bathrooms and no running water, and was criticized for not meeting basic sanitation standards. The AEC built a second school less than two years later. The old school was moved across the street to Sixth Avenue and E Street, where it was used as a social hall into 1964.

Today, the former School Reserve area is occupied by Town Square and the Alaska Center for the Performing Arts, the city's premier cultural landmark (see page 43). The center, known as "the PAC" by locals, is ringed in computer-controlled lighting and has multiple theaters, including the Evangeline Atwood Concert Hall. The school building has been preserved and was again moved after the earthquake in 1964 to its current location at Third and Eagle streets. Today it is commonly known as the Pioneer School House, a name it earned in its years as a meeting place for a civic group; it continues to be available for rental.

In November 1936, the grand opening of the ornate concrete-and-gypsum Anchorage City Hall was greeted as a sign that the city was here to stay. "One of the finest public buildings in Alaska," crowed the *Anchorage Daily Times*. Located on Fourth Avenue, a dirt road on the Municipal Reserve portion of the town site, the new city hall was home to not only the mayor's office and city council chambers, but also held a telephone office, a library, and a jail, which surely benefited from the building's eight-inch-thick walls.

The two-story building was of the classical Beaux Arts style, a nineteenth-century Parisian-influenced style distinguished by a symmetrical facade, nearly flat roof, and rusticated, or exaggeratedly patterned, masonry—as seen in the blocks around the main door's archway. Anchorage City Hall was built locally with the designs of Alaska architect E. Ellsworth Sedille—a decision lauded by the Public Works Administration, which paid half of the building costs.

In 1980, the building was restored and remodeled in the style of a 1930s-era bank and leased to the Alaska Pacific Bank Corporation. The old city hall is now on the National Register of Historic Places and has been home to the Anchorage Convention and Visitors Bureau since 1996. The current tenants moved in after a controversial eviction of the previous tenants, which included a popular art gallery and the Anchorage Concert Association. Less controversial was the 1996 renovation by Anchorage Historic Properties Inc., which redesigned the interior into one more befitting a modern office building. Official city hall business is now conducted at a utilitarian eight-story building at 632 West Sixth Avenue.

Loussac's Pharmacy at Fourth Avenue and D Street was an all-purpose store. Among other things, it's said to have been the first store to introduce avocados to Anchorage. This photo shows a parade passing in front of the pharmacy and neighboring clothiers, probably fronting Fourth Street, in 1916. Pharmacy owner Z. J. "Zack" Loussac later partnered with a former pharmacy employee, Dr. Harold Sogn, to open the New Doctor's Clinic in the Loussac-Sogn Building, which was built for that purpose; the building seen here is likely a predecessor of that venture. The Loussac-Sogn Building, built in 1947, has been called Anchorage's first medical/business office complex.

The Loussac-Sogn Building at 425 D Street is a modest landmark. Except for the small historical placards posted outside, it is an unassuming part of a retail street. Today, the name Loussac is more often associated with the main branch of the municipal library, which bears its first benefactor's name.

Today's Loussac-Sogn Building houses retail properties and offices, including a jewelry store. The simple Art Moderne style of the building blends seamlessly with its modern retail uses. It is across the street from the Fifth Avenue Mall, which was built in 1987.

The Federal Building, located between F and G streets on Fourth Avenue, was built in 1939 to house the post office, the Third District Court, and a range of federal agencies, including the Civilian Conservation Corps, the U.S. Signal Corps, and the Alaska Railroad. The original engraving on the building reads "United States Post Office and Courthouse." The poured concrete building was designed by government architect Gilbert Stanley Underwood, who was also responsible for building the first of the U.S. State Department buildings in Washington, D.C. The original federal district courtroom and post office included Depression-era Alaskan murals painted by Richard Haines and Arthur Kerrick.

Obscured by landscaping, the old Federal Building seems somewhat less imposing today. Through the entrance to the right, visitors enter Anchorage's Alaska Public Lands Information Center, one of several such museum-like education and information centers throughout the state that provide visitors with information on wildlife, camping, culture, and public lands on behalf of eight federal and state agencies. Exhibits and videos are among the offerings. The building still contains a post office, as well as a bank, on its first floor. Kerrick's mural still exists in the old courtroom. Most of today's Federal Building business has moved to the new Federal Building on C Street in midtown Anchorage, which was built between 1976 and 1980.

The Lathrop Building, a local landmark known as the home of the Art Deco–style Fourth Avenue Theater, was completed in 1947 after a five-year delay in construction during World War II. The theater was built by Cap Lathrop, who was previously responsible for a chain of theaters throughout Alaska. This three-story building was even more show-stopping inside than out, with elegant and elaborate Art Deco murals depicting the development of the state decorating the walls, and a sky of "stars" with a prominent Big Dipper adorning the ceiling. The first movie to be shown here was *The Jolson Story*. In addition to the theater, the building contained radio and television stations, offices, and a restaurant.

Immortalized in local art and memory, the Fourth Avenue Theater has become a symbol for downtown Anchorage. It survived the 1964 earthquake and became one of the city's most distinctive landmarks. Restored by the city in the mid 1980s, the Fourth Avenue Theater offered repertory performances and showed films until January 1990. It later operated as a venue for special events for a catering company. Although it continued to be a venue for Anchorage entertainment into the twenty-first century, the Fourth Avenue Theater's doors were closed in May 2006. Its future remains uncertain. The theater has been a popular cause for local historic preservationists, who have pushed for the city to buy the property. However, voters turned down a $2 million referendum to fund the purchase, and nonprofit funds to support it have not come through.

In this photograph from the late 1920s, the Alaska Railroad Band poses outdoors in what is now Town Square, with Kimball's Dry Goods in the background. Irving and Della Kimball opened their store in a wood-frame commercial building measuring forty by sixty feet on two of the original town site lots, purchased in November 1915. The store sold the basic provisions of frontier life, from coffee and kettles to guns, serving a community of hardy homesteaders. The Kimball family worked and lived in the store, which had household quarters in the back. When Irving Kimball died in 1921, Della continued the store's operation.

Kimball's Dry Goods became the oldest continuously operating store in Anchorage. Decema Kimball Andresen Slawson, who was nine when her father opened the store, joined her mother in its operation in the 1950s. Upon her mother's death, Slawson divided the building at the corner of Fifth and E into two shop spaces, renting half to the Kobuk Coffee Company. In the 1980s, Slawson spoke publicly about the building's history to help save it from destruction, which was imminent with the creation of neighboring Town Square. She continued to run Kimball's into the late 1990s as a fabric store and shared stories of old Anchorage with schoolchildren and customers. Kimball's Dry Goods closed its storefront business in 2002, months after Slawson's death at age ninety-five—she died in her home in the back of the building (inset). The Kobuk Coffee Company now owns the building and has since expanded to fill both retail spaces. Now adjoining Town Square, the lot is Anchorage's only privately owned property on municipal land.

On March 27, 1964, south-central Alaska was hit with a 9.2 magnitude earthquake, the largest to date in North America. Those who remember the "Good Friday" quake say they watched streets ripple like waves. The epicenter was just 150 miles southeast of Anchorage and hit the city's downtown area particularly hard. This view, looking west toward the Anchorage Westward Hotel, shows a broken and buckled Fourth Avenue. Anchorage was the largest community affected by the quake.

The Anchorage Westward Hotel survives as one tower of the Hilton Anchorage skyscraper complex, seen here on the far right. Buildings on the north side of Fourth Street were not recoverable and were razed, ultimately replaced with new buildings such as the Sunshine Mall (originally the Post Office Mall). The Army-Navy Surplus store, not visible in the archival photo, was one of the original pre-1964 businesses that survived. The disaster actually brought a new construction boom to town and helped the city move forward. By July 1965, more than $27 million in federal relief aid had already been designated to help Anchorage rebuild.

One of Anchorage's earliest buildings, and certainly the only one to feature anything as fanciful as a turret, the Wendler Building was built in 1915 on the original town site at Fourth Avenue and I Street. The two-story wood-frame building featuring a Victorian-style turret was operated as Larson & Wendler Groceries, with a living space upstairs for the family of co-owner A. J. Wendler. A former Valdez brewer who moved to Anchorage and changed lines of business during an early prohibition movement in Alaska, Wendler would become president of the chamber of commerce and head Anchorage's first school board. Although similarly styled buildings were known elsewhere in Alaska, including in Valdez, this building was one of a kind in Anchorage.

Still one of a kind, the Wendler Building has been transported down the street from its original location and now lends old-fashioned charm to another commercial district. Since the grocery closed, the building has hosted apartments, a restaurant, and a women's "hospitality" club—the Club 25 seen in the inset photo on the opposite page—which was later opened to both men and women. The Wendler family donated the building to the municipality in 1983 on the condition that it be preserved. The municipality moved the historic structure to its present location at Fourth Avenue and D Street against the recommendations of a relocation study that found the site unsuitable, in part due to a lack of other historic structures nearby. In front of the building is a statue of the sled dog Balto, famous for leading the team that transported diphtheria serum to Nome in 1925—the inspiration behind today's Iditarod Trail Sled Dog Race.

The "Cemetery Reserve" boundaries, which encompass Sixth and Ninth avenues and Fairbanks and Cordova streets downtown, were delineated by an executive order of President Woodrow Wilson in 1915. In 1918, President Wilson issued another executive order that authorized subdividing the land into tracts to be sold to religious or fraternal organizations—as well as lots "open to burial privileges by the public without charge for the land." Burials were performed by the tract owners as well as by the city with very little central planning. Individual tract owners were also responsible for the groundskeeping and maintenance of their plots.

Downtown bustles ever closer to the plots, as seen in this northward view with the Sheraton Hotel in the background. Through the years, the cemetery has undergone many changes, but it remains the final resting place for today's residents as well as the region's original settlers. In 1951, a portion of the original Cemetery Reserve was conditionally sold to the Alaska Housing Authority for public housing, but the apartments there were razed in 1991 and the land ownership reverted to the municipality. In February 1975, the cemetery was renamed Anchorage Memorial Park Cemetery. In April 1991, the Anchorage Memorial Park Cemetery Advisory Commission was formed to advise the mayor and the assembly on matters of policy concerning the cemetery. On April 26, 1993, the Anchorage Memorial Park Cemetery was listed in the National Register of Historic Places.

The Anchorage Daily Times Building, pictured here in 1957, on the south side of Fourth Avenue between H and I streets, was for many years home to Alaska's largest newspaper. The paper once occupied a far smaller building two blocks away. The *Times* traces its roots to 1915, when a tiny paper called the *Cook Inlet Pioneer* got its start. Two years later, through consolidation, the paper became the *Anchorage Daily Times*. By 1919, the paper was operating out of a small building on F Street between Fourth and Fifth avenues (inset).

In 1935, Bob Atwood bought the paper, which took such stances as advocating for statehood and moving the state capital from Juneau. Atwood updated the building in the late 1960s, adding windows and a more modern-looking facade that fit the architectural style of the time. The paper changed its name to the *Anchorage Times* in 1976, and Atwood sold it in 1989 to the owner of an oil services company. The paper lasted until 1992, when the competing *Anchorage Daily News* bought the *Times* and folded it.

Three years after the *Anchorage Times* folded, the Alaska court system bought the building and renamed it the Snowden Administration Building after court administrative director Art Snowden. The building has changed little since 1967, but the surrounding streets beam with a mix of old and new buildings and stores. Across from the Snowden Administration Building is the Pioneer Bar, one of the oldest taverns in the city. Less than a block down the street is the Hotel Captain Cook, built after the 1964 earthquake, and the Nesbett Courthouse, built in 1996.

By the late 1940s, Fourth Avenue in downtown Anchorage was beginning to look like Main Street America, as evident in this 1949 photograph at the corner of Fourth Avenue and E Street. A cadre of shops reflecting the uniqueness of Alaska lined the avenue—the city's main drag—including an Alaska Airlines ticket office and the Cheechako Tavern (a "cheechako" is a greenhorn, somebody who hasn't survived an Alaska winter yet). Other shops nearby included the North Pole Bakery and the Piggly Wiggly. The Hewitt's sign on the building pictured here refers to Hewitt's Drug Store. Formerly Hewitt's Photo Shop, the store became a favorite Anchorage meeting spot, known for its soda fountain and ice cream as well as a diverse array of goods. Wares included paintings by Alaska artist Sydney Laurence. On the other side of Fourth Avenue were the studios for KFQD, the first radio station in Alaska, and the old city hall.

The corner of Fourth Avenue and E Street is one of the most-photographed sites in downtown Anchorage. A vortex of gift and photo shops, eateries, and art galleries, it is popular with tourists and locals alike. Bear Square, pictured here, gives the corner the atmosphere of an open mall. Although technically a survivor of the 1964 earthquake, the Hewitt's building was torn down shortly afterward due to unstable ground—as were most of its more damaged neighbors to the east. After numerous moves, Hewitt's Drug Store relocated to an orthopedic office building in midtown, on Lake Otis Boulevard. Current owner Bob Niebert has held onto some memorabilia from the original store—including stools from the pharmacy's soda counter.

The Alaska Building, pictured here in 1956, sits on the southwest corner of Fourth Avenue between G and H streets and was one of the first buildings to go up in Anchorage. The Anchorage Museum of History and Art pegs the building's construction at 1916. In 1915, Jacob B. Gottstein came to Anchorage to sell food, tobacco, and other goods to the workers building the Alaska Railroad. The town was starting to become a small, thriving place of commerce, though it still lacked basic necessities, such as a bank. The Bank of Anchorage opened up in the Alaska Building and did business there until 1924, when Gottstein bought the building and opened J.B. Gottstein Wholesale Foods Company. In many ways, the town grew up around the Alaska Building, with the old city hall nearby, First National Bank Alaska across the street, and the former Empress Theatre next door. Over the years, other well-known businesses like Bert's Drug Store and the Bootery moved into the building, and the intersection of Fourth Avenue and G Street was one of the liveliest in town.

The Alaska Building is now owned by attorney Jim Gottstein, the grandson of J. B. Gottstein. The old family wholesale grocery store now contains law offices, a café, deli, gift shops, and a handful of nonprofit agencies, including the World Wildlife Fund's Alaska offices. In 1997, Jim Gottstein, who has his office on the second floor, installed a Webcam, known as the AlaskaCam, on the Alaska Building, one of the first Webcams of its kind in the country. The AlaskaCam still operates today, receiving thousands of hits daily and offering real-time views of Fourth Avenue. The Alaska Building has stood the test of time, surviving the Good Friday Earthquake in 1964 and a smattering of redevelopments across downtown. One of its more striking recent features has been a banner placed across the top of the building: "Raise Taxes." It's a bit of political commentary on the part of Gottstein, who believes Alaska should institute an income tax; currently, residents pay no state sales or income taxes.

The Z. J. Loussac Public Library, pictured here during its opening in June 1955, was located on the south end of Fifth Avenue and F Street. It is named in honor of the man who funded its construction. Alaska drugstore owner and philanthropist Z. J. Loussac was a Russian immigrant who came to Alaska in the early 1900s. Loussac opened his pharmacy near Fourth Avenue and E Street and was lauded for his civic involvement in Anchorage. He earned his wealth during the slim years of World War II, served three terms as mayor, and created the Loussac Foundation, which donated the library to the city. The library closed its Fifth Avenue location in 1981 and moved nearby to Sixth Avenue, a temporary location while a new building was constructed off Thirty-sixth Avenue in midtown Anchorage. The city kept the name, Z. J. Loussac Public Library, when the new building was completed in 1986. The new library (inset, opposite), which is composed of three cylinder-like brick buildings, is an intriguing modern structure.

The Egan Center, a 45,000-square-foot convention center, took over the old library site on Fifth Avenue. Named after former Alaska governor Bill Egan, the center opened in 1984 and was part of the "Project 80s" construction program funded by booming oil revenues. The Egan Center signaled the changing face of Anchorage as the oil industry prospered and the city began taking on an air of sophistication. The Egan Center has played host to large concerts and conventions over the years, including the annual gathering of the Alaska Federation of Natives, which brings more than 3,000 Eskimos, Aleuts, and Indians to town in the fall. In summer, the cruise ship companies have used the Egan Center to stage tours to Denali National Park and other attractions in the state. A new convention center is under construction two blocks west of the Egan Center. With 215,000 square feet, the $93 million Dena'ina Civic and Convention Center will increase the city's convention space by more than 300 percent. The new center is expected to be completed in 2008.

Anchorage Alaska Grade School 1939.

Central Grade School, pictured here at Fifth Avenue and F Street in 1939, was built in the late 1930s by the Public Works Administration. With its Art Deco design and long hallways, Central Grade School was part of a building boom in the late 1930s that is often referred to as the "second generation" of structures to go up in the city. The school, which replaced an old wood-frame building, held up to 800 students of all ages, a staggering capacity for a town of just 3,000 people at the time. The school's hallways, however, were soon packed with children. In the years of World War II, when the United States and Japan fought on Alaska's Aleutian Islands, the U.S. military beefed up its presence in Anchorage, building Elmendorf Air Force Base and Fort Richardson. The town's population swelled to an estimated 50,000 people, with many children attending Central Grade School. The school was later converted into the city hall annex.

The Alaska Center for the Performing Arts sits at the former site of Central Grade School and the city hall annex. F Street between Fifth and Sixth avenues is now blocked to vehicle traffic. The PAC, as locals refer to the theater complex, opened in 1988 and is one of the city's most elegant buildings, with a series of pitched roofs, tall atriums, and a parklike setting adjacent to Town Square. The 176,000-square-foot building has four performance halls, including the large Atwood Concert Hall, and plays host to Broadway musicals, international musicians, lecturers, and other performers and artists. The PAC was a $65 million project largely financed as part of the Project 80s, a public improvement program funded by soaring oil tax revenues collected by the state in the late 1970s and early 1980s. By the time the PAC opened, however, oil prices had crashed, and Anchorage was steeped in recession, with thousands of people leaving the state in the late 1980s. It took the economy several years to recover.

Military and pleasure travel to Alaska by bus predated a city transit system. By early 1942, Greyhound was planning a new bus depot in anticipation of the completion of the Alaska Highway, and announced that its expansion plans could include "a city transit service in the near future." Bus service began almost as soon as the highway was opened to public traffic in 1943, with a contract between Greyhound and the Northwest Service Command. The Anchorage City Bus Depot was located at Fourth and A streets. By the 1950s, the bus depot was bustling. Bowling lanes were among the entertainment offered to those awaiting a ride. In 1952, the Alaska Air Guard began operations with its headquarters office just above the depot.

The Alaska Fur Factory, the building's current occupant, has been in business at this location since the 1960s. The Atlas figure on top of the building is a holdover from a gym that formerly occupied the location. The original building has been refaced and undergone extensive remodeling, but some original features remain, including the carved stone street number. Tens of millions have ridden city transit, and today's bus system transports more than 12,000 commuters each day.

J.C. Penney, at the northeast corner of Fifth Avenue and E Street, was one of the first national department stores to open in Anchorage. It had been open only a short time when, on March 27, 1964, the five-story store seen here was destroyed in the Good Friday Earthquake (also known as the Great Alaska Earthquake), the most powerful temblor ever recorded in North America. With a magnitude of 9.2, the quake killed 131 people in Alaska and destroyed much of downtown, razing buildings, uprooting streets, and cutting off power and water throughout the city. The quake happened at 5:36 p.m., just as people were leaving work, and shook Anchorage for more than three minutes. Concrete slabs from the J.C. Penney building peeled from the walls and crashed to sidewalks and cars below. More than 500 customers and workers were inside the building at the time. One person was killed by the falling debris.

J.C. Penney rebuilt after the earthquake and thrived as a major downtown tenant throughout the 1970s. In the 1980s, J.C. Penney became the cornerstone of a new $67 million shopping center downtown. Opening amid a statewide recession, the Anchorage Fifth Avenue Mall struggled initially, but the five-level shopping center has since become one of the most popular hangouts in downtown, especially during the holidays and dark winters. A large dome resembling a flying saucer covers a food court on the fourth level. A sky bridge connects the mall to Nordstrom's department store at the corner of Sixth Avenue and D Street. The mall borders the emerging SoNo District, a trendy area of downtown located a block south of Nordstrom's—thus the name "SoNo."

The Delaney Park Strip, a block-wide, mile-long stretch of green space between Ninth and Tenth avenues in downtown Anchorage, has been used as a firebreak, airstrip, golf course, and military housing. One of its most famous moments took place on June 30, 1958, a date longtime Alaskans will never forget. On that day, Alaska jettisoned its reputation as "Seward's Folly" and joined the rest of the country as the forty-ninth state in the union. Congress passed the Alaska Statehood Bill, which became official on January 3, 1959, when Alaska was formally admitted into the union. "WE'RE IN," read the front-page headline in the *Anchorage Times* on June 30. At the Federal Building on Fourth Avenue, Alaskans added a forty-ninth star to a giant American flag. Meanwhile, some 25,000 Anchorage residents gathered on Delaney Park Strip and ignited a giant bonfire (inset). Fifty tons of wood were burned.

Delaney Park Strip today is a thriving greenway replete with tennis and basketball courts, ball fields, and vast stretches of open space. An old rotary snowplow locomotive, one of the last steam engines operated by the Alaska Railroad, is positioned on the park perimeter and harks back to the town's railroad roots when Anchorage was populated with workers laying tracks between Seward and Fairbanks. On breezy summer days, colorful kites the size of small airplanes hang over the park like international flags. The park also plays host to a number of festivals, including the annual Fourth of July celebration and summer concerts. Delaney Park Strip has even been the scene of an international religious gathering. In 1981, an estimated 80,000 people descended on the park to see Pope John Paul II. The monument shown here was erected to commemorate his visit.

The early years of aviation in Anchorage involved pilots landing their biplanes on what is now the Delaney Park Strip. As the city grew, it became apparent Anchorage needed a larger and safer place for the growing number of planes buzzing in the skies. In 1929, the federal government set aside Aviation Field, a formerly wooded area a mile east of present-day downtown Anchorage. Shortly after, the field was renamed for Russell Hyde Merrill, one of Alaska's aviation pioneers. Merrill was credited as the first pilot to cross the Gulf of Alaska and the first to make a night landing in Anchorage. It took an executive order from President Herbert Hoover to reclaim just over 140 acres of land on the original town site to establish the airport, which quickly became a center for the state's air transportation. Pictured here in 1931 with Mount Susitna in the background, Merrill Field was the city's main airport until the early 1950s, when Anchorage International Airport opened its gates.

Merrill Field, which lies between Sixth and Fifteenth avenues just east of downtown, is as busy as ever, with hundreds of Cessnas and other small planes taking off and landing each day. The city has grown up around the airport, with downtown to the west, a shopping center (and the Chugach Mountain range, seen in this view) to the east, neighborhoods to the south, and car dealerships and fast-food restaurants on the north side. The planes buzz low everywhere, reminding Alaskans of their aviation roots. Many residents, in fact, have their own planes and fly them out of Merrill Field. The airport serves the general aviation community as a commercial service airport operated by the municipality. Surrounding the field are businesses offering aviation training, plane rental, and sightseeing tours. In 2004, an average of more than 520 flights per day came through this airport. Alaska continues to have a very high number of pilots per capita; in 2006, according to FAA statistics, the state had 8,500 registered pilots—or more than one out of every 100 residents.

The Denali Theater, seen here in 1965, was once a complex featuring a pizza parlor, a pancake house, and the Thrifty Barber Shop, located at the far end of the building. The theater, which seated 600, anchored the neighborhood of Spenard, which began as a lumber camp. The road from the lumber camp to the tent city on Ship Creek was named Spenard Road for Joe Spenard, who was an owner of the lumber camp. It was considered one of the rougher areas of Anchorage, a red-light district that saw a great deal of drinking among its inhabitants. During construction of the Trans-Alaska Pipeline, the City of Anchorage successfully cleaned up Fourth Avenue by bulldozing dozens of buildings. The Denali Theater, however, was considered a wholesome piece of the neighborhood and was spared.

In 1999, the owners of a popular pizza joint across town decided that what Anchorage really needed was a theater pub. In 2000, the Beartooth, named after mountains in the Alaska Range near Mount McKinley, opened its doors and immediately the theater began to fill. On the theater side, you can eat a burrito and watch a classic movie for cheap. On the other side is a restaurant that serves more upscale cuisine. The neighborhood in general is a far cry from what it was during the construction of the Trans-Alaska Pipeline. Now dotted with independent bookstores and clothing and gift shops, Spenard has more of a bohemian feel.

Lake Spenard, pictured in this undated photograph, was a popular retreat for Anchorage picnickers and swimmers. In the 1920s and 1930s, the shores were mostly undeveloped and much of Anchorage lived around present-day downtown, about three miles away. Joe Spenard operated a resort on the shores of the lake. As aviation became more important to Alaska, the city began scouting out a landing place for seaplanes. Lake Spenard, connected by a canal to Lake Hood, was the preferred site, and construction began in the late 1940s on the city's first airport for seaplanes. A wooden airport tower from Yakutat, in southeast Alaska, was shipped to Lake Hood and became the airport's terminal and control tower. The airport was commissioned in 1953.

Lake Spenard and adjacent Lake Hood today comprise the busiest seaplane airport in the world, with more than 190 flights a day. Lake Hood Seaplane Base sits next to Ted Stevens Anchorage International Airport. In the summer, the skies are full of seaplanes alongside lumbering passenger jets, making for an unusually busy airspace. Lake Spenard is flanked by hotels on the east side, where locals and tourists alike congregate to watch seaplanes come and go while dining on fresh salmon and king crab. Sightseeing tour operators run planes out of Lake Hood, as do private citizens, many of whom consider airplanes as second cars.

Taken in August 1969, this is an aerial view of midtown before the big oil boom. In the early 1950s, Anchorage had two paved streets, one stoplight downtown, two small apartment buildings, and one new high school. The city also comprised the original downtown area as well as one area to the north. At the time, the population was about 11,000, with 7,000 more living in homesteads outside of the city. Therefore, most of the buildings in this picture were fairly new in 1969. They were made possible by the construction of Northern Lights Boulevard, heading toward the mountains, and the Seward Highway, the only road coming in and leading out of town. The shopping center at the right of the picture is the Sears Mall, which housed one of the first chain retail outfits in Alaska.

Seen from a slightly different vantage point, north and east of the original photo, this contemporary image shows how midtown has grown. The light square in the upper right corner is part of the Sears Mall. The "Anchorage Bowl"—the core of the city—is 100 square miles and home to about 220,000 people. The Anchorage Bowl is almost entirely surrounded by water to the west and by the Chugach National Forest to the east. Running through the city is a series of paved trails, many miles of which are through state and federal parks. This leaves little room to expand. About one-sixth of the Anchorage Bowl's total land area, or 11,700 acres, was available for development. In the late 1970s and 1980s, when the state was flush with oil money, the population grew by 140 percent and buildings arose throughout the city without much forethought. There are some exceptions, however. The high-rise seen at the upper right is the British Petroleum Building, which was built in 1982 and is considered the most sophisticated oil-era office building. The city is working on plans to rezone and redesign midtown to make it a more "walkable" area.

Pictured here in 1918, the St. Nicholas Russian Orthodox Church is the oldest building in the Anchorage area and is listed on the National Register of Historic Places. The exact year the church was built is unknown, but it was probably constructed around 1870. The log-framed building, located about twenty-five miles north of Anchorage, sits on traditional lands inhabited continually by the Athabaskan people for hundreds of years. On their arrival to Alaska, the Russians wasted no time in trying to convert Alaska natives to the Russian Orthodox religion. It's estimated that tens of thousands of Alaska natives converted, but the people held onto many of their beliefs as well.

The St. Nicholas Russian Orthodox Church sits today in what is called Eklutna Historical Park. The park displays a stunning mix of Orthodox and native Athabaskan traditions. The cemetery is an especially interesting example of native culture, with more than eighty colorful "spirit houses" built over graves. St. Nicholas Church was renovated in the mid-1950s.

The New St. Nicholas Russian Church was built next to it in 1977 (seen in background of inset photo). The churches attract tourists and locals alike and are listed in many guides. Nearby is the Mike Alex Cabin, the home of a former Eklutna tribal chief who was a member of the Russian Orthodox Church and who helped build the new church.

The Eklutna cemetery, pictured here in 1946, was a sacred burial ground for the Athabaskans who lived in the area for hundreds of years. The native people cremated their dead and built houses over the ashes. These "spirit houses," painted in family colors, held the possessions that the deceased needed for the afterlife. The Russian Orthodox Church moved into the area around 200 years ago, but the native people continued to construct spirit houses even after they were converted, although missionary influences can be seen in the crosses scattered about the graveyards. Those houses affixed with crosses mark the graves of persons who had converted to the Russian Orthodox faith.

Today, there are more than eighty spirit houses in the Eklutna cemetery, and some Athabaskan families are still placing spirit houses over their loved ones' graves. The practice, however, is rare. The Eklutna cemetery is located in Eklutna Historical Park, a popular attraction twenty-five miles north of Anchorage. Eklutna Historical Park offers visitors a blend of Russian Orthodox and native Athabaskan traditions. Close by, the St. Nicholas Russian Orthodox Church is the oldest standing building in the Anchorage area. The village of Eklutna is one of several villages that were located in the area. Now, it's the only village located in the municipality.

Anchorage International Airport opened its gates in 1953, becoming not only the state's hub airport but also a world-renowned pit stop for jets traveling between Europe, Asia, and North America. The airport was the nexus for a territory that depended on air travel to get around. With few roads in the state, Anchorage International was a critical supplier of food, mail, and other goods to Alaska's far-flung towns and cities. But that wasn't its only purpose. Few small cities could claim as many international airlines as Anchorage in the 1960s and 1970s. The bustling airport became known as the "Air Crossroads of the World" because of its unique polar location. Passenger airlines regularly refueled in Anchorage on their way to and from the Lower 48 and other countries. They could fly over the North Pole to Frankfurt in under ten hours, and reach Tokyo in seven hours, or Hawaii in under six, thus giving Anchorage a sense of international flair. That began to change in the late 1980s as long-range jets came into use and Russia opened its airspace.

In 2000, the Alaska legislature renamed the airport Ted Stevens Anchorage International Airport in honor of then-U.S. senator Ted Stevens, known by Alaskans as "Uncle Ted." At the time, the airport was undergoing a major makeover, including to the old Concourse C, which had been damaged in an earthquake and was never fully repaired. The new design, with its towering steel columns, sweeping views of the Chugach Mountains, and Alaska's first and only moving walkway, ushered Alaska aviation into the twenty-first century. Unlike the old days, however, Anchorage is no longer a major stopover for passenger jets flying between continents, mainly because longer-range aircraft don't need to refuel. But FedEx, UPS, and other air-cargo operators use the city's airport as a pit stop between Asia and the Lower 48. By landing in Anchorage, they can carry more cargo and less fuel on each leg. In fact, so many air freighters land in Anchorage that it often ranks as one of the world's busiest cargo airports.

A town tucked into Turnagain Arm, about thirty-five miles south of Anchorage, Girdwood was born just before the turn of the twentieth century as a supply post for gold mining activity in the area. Originally called Glacier City, it was renamed for James E. Girdwood, a former New York linen salesman who had gold claims in the area. Eventually, those and other claims would make up the short-lived Crow Creek Alaska Hydraulic Gold Mining Company and later the Girdwood Hydraulic Gold Mining Company. By

1917, Girdwood's Main Street had sixteen buildings, five of which were saloons. The most popular of these was the Little Dipper Inn, shown at the right in this picture. Until the time it burned down when the 1964 earthquake struck, it was the center of activity for what's now called Old Town. Not only was it the most popular bar, restaurant, and inn, it also served as a general meeting place and a post office.

The original town site is only a skeleton of its former self. A few unpaved roads mark where the old town once was. The 1964 earthquake caused Girdwood to sink along the mouth of Glacier Creek and Turnagain Arm, putting much of the town below high tide. Some of the buildings were relocated more than two miles to higher ground, around which a community began to grow. Girdwood is Alaska's premier ski resort area, a place where animals and children run freely on the streets, and where squatters live in makeshift houses alongside some of Alaska's most powerful people, including U.S. senator Ted Stevens, who has a home in Girdwood. Many Girdwood residents enjoy the small-town atmosphere that can be found here, away from the growth and development of downtown Anchorage.

In 1898, Thomas Corwin Mendenhall, an Ohio physicist and meteorologist who worked for the U.S. Coast and Geodetic Survey, recorded a glacier fifty miles south of Anchorage. The ice sheet became known as the Portage Glacier (pictured here in 1971) because it straddled the old portage route used by Russian trappers and other travelers going between the mountains of Prince William Sound and Turnagain Arm, a narrow passage off Cook Inlet.

The glacier started to form during the Little Ice Age about 400 years ago. A lake at the mouth of the glacier served as a perch for snapping pictures, and in 1986, the U.S. Forest Service opened the Begich-Boggs Visitor Center at the end of the lake. At the time, it was believed the glacier would be visible from the visitor center until at least 2020.

Since the Begich-Boggs Visitor Center opened, the Portage Glacier has retreated around the dogleg bend in the lake. In fact, since 1994 visitors at the center haven't been able to see the glacier. They must take a boat around the bend to catch a glimpse of the vanishing ice sheet. Scientists always knew the glacier would eventually retreat out of the site, but they didn't think it would happen until 2020. As with other glaciers in Alaska, the warming Arctic climate is having an effect on the old ice. Still, scientists say the Portage Glacier is retreating at a fairly natural and stable rate for a glacier exposed to lake water. Today, the Portage Glacier stretches more than four miles and is retreating at a rate of about twenty feet a year.

By the mid-1900s, Juneau's Front Street was filling in as businesses built to what was then the water's edge. The street began as a planked road. Buildings to the south (right) fronted the tide flats of Gastineau Channel, supported by pilings on the waterfront side. On the street side, sidewalk canopies gave a practical nod to Juneau's rainy climate. Signs give evidence of some of Juneau's early enterprises: beside the post office and dentist's office were pool halls, a cigar shop, and—front and center at what was then South Front Street—a bar. By the onset of nationwide prohibition in 1920, an earlier statewide prohibition known as the Alaska Bone Dry Act had transformed such businesses, at least temporarily, into tearooms and soda shops.

This block between Seward Street and South Franklin, along Front, is now paved and on solid ground, supported by tailings from the Juneau rock dump, which were used as fill. Egan Drive marks the waterfront today. The area around Front and South Franklin streets has retained its reputation for vibrant nightlife, with a variety of bars, restaurants, and movie theaters, though with the added distinction of being in the heart of today's Juneau Downtown Historic District. Bookstores, art galleries, and clothing and tourist shops share space with drugstores and fast-food restaurants. The concrete Hellenthal Building, seen here at left, was built in 1916 and has been home to the First National Bank since 1925. The building beside the old post office, which formerly housed a confectionery, barbershop, and bar, burned in 1923. The space is now occupied by the Blomgren Building. The Seward Building (1913) at the end of the street houses galleries and shops.

First National Bank Bldg. Erected 1899.
This Bank carries over one million dollars in deposits.

The Lewis Building, a two-story wood-frame building at the corner of Front and Seward streets, was built in the 1890s to house the First National Bank, which moved there from Main Street. Despite the name, the bank was actually Juneau's third. After a fire in June 1924 did serious damage, the bank moved business operations down the street to the Hellenthal Building.

Behind the bank, along Seward Street, stands the five-story Goldstein Emporium, a commercial concrete building built in 1914. In addition to serving as home to a department store and fur business, the imposing building also served briefly as the territorial capitol and, from 1925 to 1931, housed the office of Governor George Parks.

Both landmark buildings still stand. The Lewis Building was renovated in 1985 and restored with attention to its former decorative touches. Today's main occupant is McDonald's. The distinctive Goldstein Building already housed multiple businesses and offices when it was engulfed by a fire in 1939—a blaze stoked by winds so fierce that citizens worried it might take the rest of the business district with it. With a 1945 renovation, the building has survived to house retail and office space, from fast-food restaurants to an acupuncture clinic. Fires continue to threaten Juneau's historic buildings, many of which are built of wood and lack fire-suppressing sprinkler systems.

Well into the 1930s, the Nugget Shop Building housed apartments as well as its namesake shop, which offered among its merchandise gold nuggets and local art, including baskets woven by Native Americans and paintings by the artist Sydney Laurence. Owned by Dr. Robert Simpson and Miss Minnie Goldstein, the shop had formerly been housed at the Seward Building at Front and Franklin but moved in 1923. One 1928 newspaper account documents the arrival of "The Old Witch totem pole from Sukkwan," at the time said to be "about 100 years old."

The totems are gone, but an Alaska-themed gift shop still anchors this building firmly in Juneau's tourist scene at today's new address, South Franklin Street and Ferry Way. Owner May George Jefford worked in the old Nugget Shop as a teenager. After her family moved to Anchorage in the 1940s, she comanaged a gift shop there with her mother. With more than fifty years in the business, Jefford now runs multiple gift-shop chains, including Once in a Blue Moose. The store offers a variety of souvenirs, including pottery, T-shirt novelties, and ulus (curved knives used in the Alaskan bush), which Jefford has been credited with introducing to tourists.

As early as 1894, when Alaska was not yet a territory, the federal government was entertaining recommendations that Alaska's capital be moved from Sitka to Juneau "because of its location, population and wealth." It would be decades before the capitol, or even a representational local government, would become reality. At first, unsure they even wanted a legislature, Alaskans vigorously campaigned for local rule after President William Taft suggested the alternative would be a territory governed by appointees from a distance. A partial

congressional appropriation for the Federal and Territorial Building first came in 1911. It took donations from a frustrated citizenry to get the $800,000 project underway. Governor George A. Parks opened Alaska's Capitol Building on February 2, 1931. The building features four columns of marble quarried in southeast Alaska. In addition to the legislature, the building originally housed government offices, including a post office, and a radio office, where locals made their long-distance phone calls until citywide service started in 1939.

The capitol looks mostly unchanged, but it serves a much larger constituency. The legislature consists of a forty-member house of representatives and a twenty-member senate, and convenes for a 120-day regular session beginning in January, plus additional special sessions as called by the governor and legislature. The Liberty Bell replica in front of the capitol came from the U.S. Treasury Department as part of a 1950 Independence Savings Bond drive. The Masonic building just behind the capitol still stands, as does the building at the left, which today houses the Juneau-Douglas City Museum. Perennial public debate over moving the state's center of government is fueled by the changing natures of commerce, communication, and transportation. The state's wealthiest and most populous city is Anchorage—more centrally located than Juneau and reachable on the road system. Supporters of keeping government in Juneau, however, might also point out the growing possibilities of the Internet, which the state is increasingly using to serve its constituents.

In 1912, while Congress was putting the final touches on the bill to make Alaska a territory and Juneau its capital, Alaska's first territorial government building, the Governor's Mansion, was already in progress. The supervising architect of the U.S. Treasury, James Knox Taylor, designed the building in the last year of his fifteen-year tenure. The final product was simplified from his original plans, which called for a partly brick exterior as well as numerous decorative touches, such as low-relief designs on the walls, pilasters made to look like columns, and parquet floors. Builders modified his plans to meet a $40,000 budget and produced a comparatively modest 12,900-square-foot frame building. The mansion's first official public event was an open house reception on New Year's Day 1913. Walter Eli Clark, Alaska's district governor since 1909, was the first to live in the house with his family while serving out his four-month term as Alaska's first territorial governor from January to April 1913.

Fronting Calhoun Avenue and just around the corner from the State Office Building and the capitol, as of 2007 the Governor's Mansion has been home to eleven governors and their families during statehood, as well as eleven territorial (or acting territorial) governors in the years before statehood. Now a 14,400-square-foot building, the mansion has been remodeled numerous times, including a $2.5 million renovation in the 1980s. However, Taylor would still recognize his creation, since some of the first changes, done in the 1930s, were designed to restore his original vision of a white plaster Greek Revival–style building. Later changes brought in modern conveniences such as heating. In 2007, the incoming governor, Sarah Palin, a Republican and Alaska's first female governor, became the state's first "commuter governor," choosing not to stay at the mansion year-round. Palin made news by announcing she would stay at her Wasilla home until the legislature convened in January, in order to avoid disrupting her children's schooling.

The first Russian Orthodox church in Juneau was founded on the support and vision of the local community of Tlingit, an Alaska indigenous people with settlements along the southeast coast. Eastern Orthodox influence in Alaska dates to the first days of Russian occupation in the 1700s. Most of Sitka's Tlingit population had already converted, in great part due to the church's practice of offering services in the Tlingit language. In 1892, when Auke

Chief Yees Gaanaalx and his wife converted, hundreds of Tlingit from this Juneau region followed suit. Native leaders told Sitka's Bishop Nikolai they had been inspired by dreams of a white-bearded man who looked like images of St. Nicholas. Work on the church began in 1893. The church was built by Tlingits, who donated labor and land to the effort, as well as local miners, including many Slavs. The church was consecrated in June 1894.

Perched atop a residential crossroads at Fifth and Gold streets above Juneau's downtown, the small octagonal building topped with an onion-shaped dome remains an unmistakable landmark. It is the oldest continuously operating church of its kind in southeast Alaska. From outside, the church buildings look much the same as they did in the late nineteenth century, but keeping the church in functioning condition is an ongoing job. A 1976 restoration was supported partly with federal and state funds, as the building is now on the National Register of Historic Places. In 1989, the church's worn onion dome was resurfaced and updated; today's gleam comes not from gold leaf but automotive paint, which was deemed to be less expensive and longer-lasting than gold leaf. In 2007, an emergency appeal was under way to repair the bell tower, which had been weakened by carpenter ants. The house of worship still offers regular services, sung in Tlingit, Old Church Slavonic, and English.

In the shadow of Mount Juneau, the "Catholic Block" encompasses the sites of Juneau's first Catholic church and its first public hospital. This photo, taken sometime between 1910 and 1919, shows St. Ann's Hospital, a staff residence, the Church of the Nativity, a chancellery, and a school building. A fence from the neighboring Russian Orthodox Church is visible in the lower left corner. Father John Althoff, a Canadian priest given responsibility for missions in Alaska, was given the task of establishing the first chapel and living quarters on this site in 1885 for the Canadian Catholic order of the Sisters of Saint Ann, from British Columbia. The next year, the sisters opened their first hospital, serving miners and their families. The order rebuilt the church in 1910, and its hospital soon after. The order was also responsible for the Our Lady of the Mines Church and School in Douglas in 1895 and the Douglas St. Ann's Hospital.

St. Ann's Hospital continued to provide health care to the Juneau community into the late 1960s, until costs proved too high for the church to support the services. Voters approved a $4.9 million, seventeen-acre public facility, the current Bartlett Hospital. The Roman Catholic Cathedral of the Nativity of the Blessed Virgin Mary remains a center of the Catholic faith in Juneau, and by 2007, it was one of eleven Juneau parishes and nine missions in a diocese officially formed in 1951. The parish is thriving, but the church building is in distress, suffering from a failing concrete foundation and walls that have been eaten by carpenter ants. A committee is researching the possibility of a new cathedral and hopes to preserve four original 1913 stained glass windows. Since 2006, the St. Ann's parish hall has also been serving as a temporary house of worship for members of neighboring Holy Trinity Episcopal Church, which was burned by arson. St. Ann's Nursing Center, the four-story building behind the church, was built in the 1950s and operated into the mid-1990s.

In a scene anchored by Mount Troy across Gastineau Channel, this 1940s view of apartments in Juneau shows a city that has emerged from frontier living to modern apartment life. The Channel Apartments, which were built immediately after World War II on land reclaimed during the war, are at the center of the photo, with warehouse and dock operations on the left.

The area to the left is the subport, an Army facility built during the war. Willoughby Avenue makes a bend through the residences and along the docks. Built in 1935, the original Juneau-Douglas Bridge spans Gastineau Channel, connecting Juneau with Douglas Island.

Apartment life appears to have pushed the waterfront ever farther away in this view overlooking Gastineau Channel, as seen from the Calhoun Street Viaduct pedestrian bridge and stairway. Most of Willoughby Avenue is obscured by buildings. To the immediate right is a sixty-seven-unit apartment building for independent senior citizens, who value the proximity to public transportation, shopping, and government offices; the State Office Building parking garage is seen on the left. The senior residences, owned and operated by the Tlingit-Haida Regional Housing Authority, help serve the state's elderly population, which is growing faster than in any other state in the country. A new Juneau-Douglas Bridge, wider and without the towering framework of the original, was built in 1981 in roughly the same location.

U.S. Coast Guard Revenue cutters *Northland* and *Unalga* are tied up at the government dock in this 1930s scene. During World War I, the *Unalga* had, like other Coast Guard vessels, been placed under the direction of the U.S. Navy, but mainly carried mail and supplies, aided vessels in distress, and provided medical aid. It also patrolled to enforce a 1911 fur seal protection convention between the United States, Great Britain, Japan, and Russia. The *Northland* served to enforce laws and save lives in Alaskan waters.

The government dock was a float, built in the 1930s off of Femmer's Dock with the permission of businessman David Femmer. It was located near the intersection of today's Egan Drive and Willoughby Avenue; at the time, the waterfront followed along what is now Willoughby Avenue. The mountain to the left is part of Douglas Island, and the Federal Court Building is in the upper right.

The arrival of war transformed Juneau's waterfront. In May 1942, President Roosevelt transferred authority of the government dock to the U.S. Navy. Within another two weeks, the Japanese bombed Alaska's Dutch Harbor. By August 1942, the Juneau government float, Femmer's Dock, and the surrounding property had been taken over by the government. In 1943, the U.S. Army Corps of Engineers filled in acres of land with tailings from the Alaska Juneau Mine, and the government built a subport that included a military warehouse and supply center. Incidentally, in 1944, the *Northland* was responsible for the first U.S. naval capture of World War II, off of Greenland. The Federal Court Building has been replaced by the State Office Building; it no longer overlooks the waterfront, as the tidelands have been filled. Current marine traffic consists of fishing vessels, shipments of wood harvested from forests to be processed, steamer and barge service, and, of course, frequent cruise ships. The subport area is currently being redeveloped.

This waterfront scene from 1938 shows the former Federal Court Building—which housed Juneau's courthouse—perched on a promontory known for many years as Courthouse Hill, looking out onto Gastineau Channel and Douglas Island. The first courthouse, a wood-frame building also on Courthouse Hill, was destroyed in a fire in January 1898 after a lamp exploded in the office of a deputy U.S. marshall. Local residents helped save furnishings and court records. The court building was rebuilt in 1904.

A photo caption identifies the houses on pilings as the "Indian Village," a reference to the Auk Tlingit village that once occupied the shoreline from the base of Courthouse Hill to Gold Creek. The neighborhood was the site of a culturally important summer village that predated Juneau. At around the time of this photo, the city had already begun to encroach upon the edges of the Juneau Indian Village, as the former waterfront was filled in for business ventures and a new government dock.

The city's waterfront has been extended by years of expansion, and the courthouse was torn down in the 1960s to make room for today's State Office Building. Though lacking the elegance of the old courthouse, today's State Office Building, seen here from Willoughby Avenue along the former waterfront, houses not only bureaucratic offices but also offers regular free lunchtime concerts by the unusual Kimball Theater Organ located in the entry hall opposite the State Historical Library. The pipe organ, originally built to accompany silent films in the Coliseum Theatre on South Franklin Street in 1928, was later housed at the Twentieth Century Theater on Front Street before being moved to its current location in 1977. The area around the State Office Building today is a mix of businesses and private residences, including historic homes, many of which are owned by the state and are slated for eventual destruction. Only a small portion of the old Juneau Indian Village remains. The buildings that are left are no longer waterfront property, but the remaining neighborhood is recognized as a historic site.

The building of a breakwater for Harris Harbor began in late 1938, the year of this photo. Locals remember the residential area behind the boats as part of "the Flats," which was the name for a neighborhood encompassing the tideflats region west of Gold Creek. The U.S. Army Corps of Engineers supervised the effort to construct the long-awaited small-boat harbor, which was built with the help of money from the War Department. According to a newspaper account, the project would require 70,000 cubic yards of rock for the breakwater. The $320,000 total project cost for the harbor was divided, with the City of Juneau expected to pay less than one-third.

In a town where many former waterfront properties are now on land, this is one case where the waterfront won. The houses on pilings seen in the archival photo have been identified by former residents as what used to be the houses along Ninth and Tenth streets. Harris Harbor, just north of the Juneau-Douglas Bridge, is one of three small-boat harbors now operated by the City of Juneau. The harbor can accommodate 275 vessels and includes a seaplane hangar. Richard T. Harris was one of the two gold-mining founders of Juneau, and the original town site was named Harrisburgh, a name changed by the post office in 1882.

The City Cafe on South Franklin Street originally opened its doors in 1912 at a dockside location at 460 South Franklin Street. Operated by Shonosuke Tanaka and his family, the City Cafe was a favorite meeting place for locals, who appreciated its friendly management and long hours as much as its food. During World War II, the owners were forced to leave Juneau, along with other Japanese-American citizens and Japanese resident aliens, to report to an internment camp. Before the Tanaka family left, the local high school granted an early one-person graduation ceremony for the owner's son, John Tanaka, who'd excelled at his studies. After the war, Shonosuke Tanaka offered a partnership to former Seattle resident Tsamu "Sam" Taguchi, then gave him the restaurant. Taguchi restored the place, and then relocated in 1964 to another building across the street, at 439 South Franklin.

After Sam Taguchi sold his business in 1982, the second City Cafe location became a gift shop, as did Taguchi's next venture—another South Franklin Street restaurant, Taguchi's Fine Chow. Today, the original City Cafe building is gone, replaced by a parking lot and the terminal for the Mount Roberts Tramway, which transports visitors to an alpine viewpoint 1,800 feet up. At street level, the City Cafe's old neighborhood is now flooded with gift shops designed to appeal to the tourists who pour down the street from the nearby cruise ship terminal. The tram offers respite in the form of awe-inspiring views of Gastineau Channel, Douglas Island, and the Chilkat Mountains. Before the tram's completion in 1996, one would have had to make a daylong hike in order to enjoy these views.

Pacific S.S. Co's Dock. Juneau, Alaska. 2-10-26.

By the 1920s, Juneau had become a regular stop for steamers transporting supplies, such as gasoline and lumber, as well as passengers—a number of them tourists who were lured by the romance of the gold rush. Local newspaper pages of the time were filled with ads announcing ship sailings between Juneau and Seattle. This 1926 photo shows the Pacific Steamship Company dock, with the Alaska-Juneau Mine to the right. The Alaska-Juneau Mine was formed shortly after Juneau's first gold discovery in 1880 by city founders Joe Juneau and Richard Harris. After the competing Alaska-Gastineau Mine closed in June 1921 due to cave-ins, locals began debating the city's financial future. Little did they suspect that the visitors themselves would someday be the source of a new, profitable industry for Juneau.

With increasing competition, the Pacific Steamship Company made its last run to Juneau in 1933. The Alaska-Juneau Mine remained profitable until 1941, then was closed by the federal War Production Board in 1944. Today, Juneau is a popular stop for Alaska Inside Passage cruises, with hundreds of ships docking each season. This rare view of the dock in summer without a cruise ship parked in front of it at Marine Park shows what tourists who enter the city in these enormous vessels would see as they approach the shore. When cruise ships dock here, passengers on the upper levels can look directly into the windows of the library, which sits atop a city parking garage (the tall building at the right).

This view of Mount Juneau shows the original 2,701-foot Juneau-Douglas Bridge, which spanned Gastineau Channel from 1935 on. The exact year of this photo is unknown. The towering steel structure was built to join Juneau with Douglas, a mining community established in 1881 that at one time seemed destined to outpace Juneau in growth. Before the bridge, ferry service was the main mode of transportation between the two communities; the ferry service was soon discontinued after the bridge opened to traffic. Conceived by a New York industrial designer (who was likely unfamiliar with the force of Juneau winds), the span was funded by the Public Works Administration for $225,000 and its construction was supervised by the Alaska Road Commission.

Today's bridge is leaner and more streamlined than its predecessor. The Juneau-Douglas Bridge was rebuilt in 1981, and its dedication was presided by Governor Jay Hammond on October 13, the anniversary of the original bridge's inauguration. In public remarks, Hammond recalled the old bridge as a "horizontal Eiffel Tower." The city of Douglas has been unified with the city of Juneau since 1970, and now, about a third of Juneau residents live either downtown or on Douglas Island. Today's Juneau-Douglas Bridge provides vehicle and pedestrian access for these residents, as well as for visitors to Mendenhall Glacier. For a time during the construction of the new bridge, two bridges spanned Gastineau Channel; the original was demolished after the current bridge opened.

In 1962, the U.S. Forest Service built the first visitors' center in the Forest Service system, which was even then expected to welcome as many as 23,000 visitors annually. One of the Mendenhall Glacier's earliest tourists was naturalist John Muir, who wrote of his visit in his 1879 book *Travels in Alaska*. Muir called the icy formation Auk Glacier, a Tlingit name, and apparently got his glimpse by boat while leaving Juneau. The glacier had already begun its retreat in the mid-1700s, melting faster than it flowed forward. The glacier was renamed in 1892 to honor noted scientist Thomas Corwin Mendenhall, who served on the Alaska Boundary Commission, which was responsible for surveying the Alaska-Canada boundary.

One of thirty-eight large glaciers that make up the Juneau Icefield, the Mendenhall Glacier is enjoyed by visitors for its impressive presence and ease of access. The glacier is the area's top attraction and is an easy thirteen-mile drive from downtown Juneau. Carving through Mendenhall Valley, the glacier's face rises 100 feet and stretches a mile and a half wide. Its three-century-long retreat is expected to continue, particularly in light of current warming trends. By 1999, an exhibit gallery and theater were added, and more than 250,000 people visit each year to see the glacier and visitors' center.

Lights o' Juneau

Electric lights first dazzled Juneau in 1894, fourteen years after Thomas Edison invented the incandescent light bulb. A newspaper article from September 1894 commented on the new network of lights, made possible by a company formed by meat merchant Willis Thorp: "Juneau is now a metropolitan city since the advent of two large wharves and a very complete and satisfactory electric light system. The lights were turned on by the Alaska Electric Light and Power Company last Thursday and operated without a flicker." Thorp installed a water wheel and electric generator on the banks of Gold Creek to supply electricity to the city. Later power sources included a steam plant and the Sheep Creek and Nugget Creek hydroelectric plants. This photo taken around 1930 shows the city alight, with the Alaska-Juneau Mine—the heart of the town's mining industry—on the right.

This panoramic view shows Juneau's waterfront today, the bridge to Douglas Island (far left), and—to the right of the South Franklin Street Dock—the ruins of the Alaska-Juneau Mine, which closed in 1944. These days, Juneau is Alaska's top tourist destination, largely due to the hundreds of cruise ships it welcomes every summer. Gold still plays a major role in the town's wealth, from the jewelry stores lining its streets to the continued fascination with Juneau's gold rush history, which has prompted tours of the mine ruins and the site of the original gold discovery along Gold Creek. Today, cruise ships in port have been known to use surplus hydroelectric power supplied by the Alaska Electric Light and Power Company.

Alaska Territorial Fish Hatchery - Juneau -

Early concerns over salmon stocks spawned southeast Alaska's first hatcheries in the early 1900s. By territorial law, canneries were required to run hatcheries as early as 1901. About fifteen sprung up around southeast Alaska, but many of the private enterprises appeared to lack the know-how to produce the desired results, according to various accounts by the fisheries' historians. The Alaska Territorial Fish Hatchery in Juneau was the territory's first salmon hatchery. Started in 1919 by A. J. Sprague, former superintendent of an Oregon hatchery, the Juneau hatchery was located at the Arctic Brotherhood Building. In 1921, with fishermen in southeast Alaska experiencing their worst catches in fifteen years after record highs, a newspaper story announcing the hatchery's release of 16 million humpback and coho salmon fry and eggs was surely received with a mix of skepticism and hope. The hatchery's results were mixed. It closed in April 1923, and its equipment was salvaged for use at a new hatchery in Ketchikan.

Salmon and visitors alike come to the Macaulay Salmon Hatchery in large numbers—salmon, responding to biological urge to return to their home "stream," and visitors, to enjoy the spectacle of fish leaping up the hatchery's man-made fish ladder, complete with an underwater viewing window. The $7.4 million hatchery, owned by Douglas Island Pink and Chum, Inc., was built in 1989 as the Gastineau Hatchery. Its name was changed with the untimely death in 2000 of founder Ladd Macaulay, who pioneered the private nonprofit approach to hatcheries in Alaska. Located near Salmon Creek, the Macaulay Salmon Hatchery is permitted to incubate more than 111 million chum, 50 million pink, 1.5 million coho, and 700,000 chinook salmon annually. "Enhancement programs" to bolster specific stocks of fish are supported by a mix of state and federal funding. The Ladd Macaulay Visitor Center offers tours and exhibits, including an aquarium.

With commercial fishing for halibut, salmon, and black cod a growing part of the southeast Alaska economy, fishermen couldn't always depend on convenient icebergs to keep catches fresh all the way to Seattle or Vancouver. The Juneau Fish and Ice Company built the Juneau Cold Storage Plant in 1913 to fill the demand, as part of an early private-public partnership arranged through the efforts of local entrepreneur Oliver Drange and lawyer John Malone. The Juneau Fish and Ice Company built the plant with the assistance of the City of Juneau in exchange for offering space for the fire department and free public use of some facilities. When it opened, the plant was capable of freezing about 2,000 salmon a day. The successful venture expanded its facilities in 1927 and 1928. It remained a public fixture and a major source of employment in the community for decades. This view from the dockside building, likely from the 1930s, shows workers unloading fish with the mill of the Alaska-Juneau Mine in the background.

The former industrial waterfront district now caters largely to cruise ship visitors, who can enjoy shopping or riding the Mount Roberts Tramway for an eagle's-eye view of the city—all within easy walking distance of the dock. The importance of a continuing fishery is evident with the Taku Wild Alaska Seafood storefront at 505 South Franklin Street, which opened as Taku Smokeries in 1984, shortly after the Juneau Cold Storage Plant closed. The company processes and sells smoked and fresh frozen seafood, including halibut, salmon, and king crab. A 1987 fire destroyed the cold storage building, which by then was no longer in business, and it was demolished. The Juneau Cold Storage Plant's dock has since been modified and upgraded to accommodate cruise ships (inset). Briefly in the late 1990s, the former plant site was home to an Alaska native-themed summer theater group. The Alaska-Juneau Mine closed in 1944 due to World War II; today, its buildings lie in ruin, and are obscured by vegetation in this picture.

The Tee Harbor Packing Cannery represented some of the earliest local efforts at finding wealth in natural resources other than gold. The first cannery began operations here in 1911. According to a newspaper report, that cannery doubled its capacity in 1914. In 1921, the cannery packed about 30,000 cases of fish, most of which was red salmon from the Lynn Canal. The Tee Harbor area was also favored by locals as a pleasant spot for fishing, blueberry picking, and other recreation.

The cannery is no longer in operation. The multiple buildings that made up the Tee Harbor plant, including workers' living quarters and a mess hall, were destroyed in a 1924 fire. The total estimated loss of $400,000 included "20,000 cases of this season's pack," according to a local newspaper account the next day. The relative remoteness of Tee Harbor, located about eighteen miles north of Juneau, is a prize people will pay for today. Waterfront real estate properties in the Auke Bay/Tee Harbor district is highly desirable and is among the area's most expensive. The small natural harbor also offers a favorite anchorage for locals, who still enjoy coming here for recreation.

Founded in 1901 by gold prospectors and incorporated in 1903, the city of Fairbanks in Alaska's interior swelled in population from about five people to more than 3,000 in-town dwellers—and more than 6,000 in the area—in less than ten years. In these boom years, it was a place of taverns and held a wide mix of ethnicities and cultures. In 1918, when this photo was taken, the price of gold had dropped and so had production, and World War I had taken away many of the residents of Fairbanks. However, by that time, the town had established itself enough to have churches, schools, and a hospital, and was a permanent home to many. This view of Fairbanks shows what was then called Front Street, and is now First Avenue. The Immaculate Conception Church, to the right, was built in 1904 and moved to its current site (inset, opposite) in 1911.

With a population of more than 80,000 living in the city and surrounding areas, Fairbanks is the most populated area in the interior region of Alaska, and the second-largest in the state. Where once it was a city dominated by the gold mining industry and businesses catering to it, it's now an important trading, transportation, military, service, supply, and educational center. The government-services sector, including the military, employs more than one-third of the region's workers, and its tourism industry is booming. The city's downtown reflects this maturation. It offers coffee shops, quaint restaurants, and art galleries. Hotels, like the Marriott's SpringHill Suites (to the right of center) now take the place of taverns. Bike paths line a much-tamed river. Fairbanks calls itself "the Golden Heart of Alaska," which is as much a reference to the character of its people as it is to the discovery of gold.

In the summer of 1967, the Chena River, which had once provided the means by which Fairbanks evolved into the main hub in Alaska's interior, escaped its banks. The flood resulted in the worst—and most expensive—natural disaster in the town's history. Four people were killed, there was $85 million in property damage, and about 15,000 people were forced to evacuate. The *Fairbanks Daily News-Miner*, which was located in the building in the center of this photo, was without electricity and didn't publish for a week. Samson Hardware, on the far left, a Fairbanks institution since 1904, was flooded and condemned shortly thereafter. The Catholic-run St. Joseph's Hospital, next to the Immaculate Conception Church at right, was forced to close due to the flood. Samson Hardware's original building, dating back to 1904, was condemned in part due to flood damage.

Congress took notice of the flood's effects on Fairbanks and Fort Wainwright and authorized the construction of the $256 million flood control project. Engineers selected a site between the city of North Pole, outside of Fairbanks, and Eielson Air Force Base where the Chena River meanders within about eight miles of the Tanana River. The Chena River Lakes Flood Control Project allows managers from the U.S. Army Corps of Engineers to dam water from the Chena during periods of high flow and divert it toward the Tanana. A large city could fit inside the 20,000-acre flood control complex in North Pole, which has saved Fairbanks from flooding several times. It's the northernmost flood control project operated by the Corps of Engineers. The town hasn't been besieged by a flood since. Samson Hardware rebuilt in its previous location, just to the east of the bridge.

On November 10, 1903, an election was held to decide if Fairbanks should be incorporated. The residents believed that Fairbanks was sufficiently established and that they should be given the responsibility to provide for their own daily community functions. The first school opened shortly thereafter, housing one teacher and thirteen students. More space was soon needed. Another school, built in 1907, was seventy-six by sixty-four feet, two stories high, and had a basement. In 1907, about 150 students were enrolled. This photograph shows the school's teachers and pupils in 1908. On December 4, 1932, Fairbanks' only school burned to the ground, forcing 340 children to attend classes in temporary classrooms at the Moose Hall, the American Legion Hall, and Eagles Hall. A little more than a year later, construction of the new building began on the site of the original school. An Art Deco style was chosen, following the design of the recently completed Federal Building in Fairbanks.

When the new school, called Main School, was completed in 1934, it had thirty-three rooms, a large basement, and a 4,000-square-foot gymnasium, which was the largest in the state. It was considered the most modern school facility in the Territory of Alaska. In 1976, it closed its doors as a public school and became the home of the administration offices of the Fairbanks North Star Borough School District. The building fell into disrepair, and by 1992, it was on the Alaska Association for Historic Preservation's list of the ten most endangered historic properties. In 1993, the school district offices moved out of the building. Main School was boarded up and the heat turned off. Then, in December 1994, several city offices moved into the building. On their own time, city employees did basic renovation in some rooms and hallways, and Main School began the transformation into what is now Fairbanks City Hall. On January 8, 1996, the mayor and city council held their first meeting in the newly completed council chambers.

The founder of Fairbanks, E. T. Barnett, was prescient in his vision of Fairbanks as a bustling gold-rush town. He was, however, off the mark when he erected his trading post, a cabin plus six-foot-high walls for a small warehouse on a one-acre site on the riverbank between what is now Cushman Street and Barnette Street, on the south side of the Chena River. In July 1902, gold was discovered in the hills north of the trading post, and the word spread quickly.

With the settlement to the south and the gold to the north of the river, the town was plagued by the annual springtime flooding of the Chena River and the subsequent washing out of the original wooden bridge, which needed to be rebuilt each year. This 1917 photo shows the construction of the all-steel bridge at Cushman Street, which the Alaska Road Commission built to replace the old wooden piling bridge. The bridge was in use until 1960.

In 1960, a concrete-and-steel bridge, seen here at the far right, was built to span the north and south parts of Fairbanks. At the time, it was called a "Span of Progress." The original 1917 bridge was moved to Nome, where it's still used today. On today's bridge, all fifty states are represented by their state flags, which were raised to celebrate Alaska's twenty-fifth year of statehood. To expedite traffic, the city has plans to build another bridge across the Chena River just west of the existing bridge. The current bridge would also be rebuilt to meet the state's seismic-related construction codes, widen driving lanes and sidewalks, and allow it to be better prepared for one-way traffic. Like any other plan to modernize downtown, this one is currently being hotly debated by the famously contrarian residents of Fairbanks.

In 1904, Fairbanks' first Catholic church, Immaculate Conception, was built by Father Francis Monroe, who by all accounts was a brave and hearty man. Almost immediately after his arrival from Eagle, Alaska, he began building the church in the Fairbanks area. He gathered funds by soliciting from gold camp to gold camp. He also talked the men in the community into helping him build the church, which was on the south side of the river. In 1906, the town decided it also needed a hospital and put Father Monroe in charge of gathering the funds to build it. The hospital was built near an old sawmill on the north side of the Chena River, near Cushman Street. As the church was on the south side and the distance between the two made attending to both the sick and the parishioners difficult, Father Monroe decided to move the church across the river, using planks and logs and horses. It was quite an event in Fairbanks, with nearly everyone coming out to watch and many placing bets against its success.

Although there were some alterations of the structure, the church still stands where it was placed in 1906 and looks much like it did then. Inside the Immaculate Conception Church, visitors are greeted with decorative tin on the ceilings and walls, a relative novelty in the northern regions of the state, as were the stained glass windows, installed in 1926. However, St. Joseph's Hospital, which was beside the church, is now occupied by the the Denali State Bank building. Its fate was sealed in the flood of 1967, when it became waterlogged. The view shown in the archival photo is today obscured by trees (see above).

The Fourth of July was a time of big celebrations in Fairbanks, and parades on what was originally called Front Street were popular events. Past the bleachers on the left is the Nordale Hotel, built by hotel magnate Tony Nordale of Dawson City in 1908. The Nordale was considered the finest hotel in Fairbanks at the time, but it burned down in 1923. Within a year, Nordale bought another building on Second Avenue, but fire consumed that building as well. Just across First Avenue from the Nordale's riverbank site was the Model Cafe. There was quite a rivalry between the restaurants in early Fairbanks until 1919, when fire once again destroyed every building from Barnette Street to Lacey Street.

Front Street, now called First Avenue, barely resembles the street that was once filled with restaurants and bars, music and drinking. Now, the street is relatively tame, lined with fine hotels, parks, bike paths, and stores. The crown jewel of the street, roughly where the Nordale Hotel used to be, is the Rabinowitz Alaska State Courthouse. The building, which opened its doors in 2001, is a $23 million state-of-the-art structure of showy glass and granite with a neon sculpture made up of ribbons of light that mimics the grandeur of the aurora borealis. The courthouse is named after the late Jay Rabinowitz, who is best remembered as a longtime chief justice of the Alaska Supreme Court.

Fairbanks was certainly a rough-and-tumble mining town. However, various "respectable" fraternal clubs, including the Eagles, the Arctic Brotherhood, the Odd Fellows, the Bohemians, the Century Club, and the Freemasons, added propriety to the town's social scene as well as its landscape. Built in 1906, the Masonic Temple was purchased from the Tanana Commercial Company in 1908 and was renovated for use as a club, with additions that included another story. When the building was extensively remodeled in 1916, the false front was added. Other additions included carpeting from Belgium and furniture from San Francisco. The *Fairbanks Daily News*, in a story about the renovation plans, said the furniture would be "luxurious" and the main halls "the prettiest in the city," which by many accounts proved to be the case. The lower part of the building was a rental, and at various times served as a school, courthouse, and shelter. The founder of Fairbanks, E. T. Barnette, lived next door.

The Masonic Temple is now on the National Register of Historic Places. It has become too expensive for the Masons to maintain, as it needs structural repair and new utility work to meet building codes, so the Masons recently moved their offices to another part of town. They're currently trying to sell the temple, and the city is committed to keeping the building intact. Next door, E. T. Barnette's former residence is now the Christian Science Reading Room. When the first Christian Science service was held in Fairbanks in 1906, two members of the congregation walked twelve miles through temperatures fifty degrees below zero in order to attend. In 1959, the church was moved to its present location.

The Lacey Street Theater was built in 1939 and was one of a string of movie theaters owned by Austin E. "Cap" Lathrop, who was considered Alaska's first home-grown millionaire. It was also one of two theaters in Fairbanks, the other one being the Empress Theater, which was across the street from the Lacey and showed what were considered at the time to be higher-quality movies. Lathrop, who owned both theaters, was a huge influence on Fairbanks and other Alaska towns as the owner of the Healy River Coal Mine, the Bank of Fairbanks, KFAR radio, and the *Fairbanks Daily News-Miner*. The Lacey Theater was (and still is) considered one of the finest pieces of architecture in Fairbanks.

Rebuilt after a fire in 1966 with minimal changes to the exterior, the Lacey Street Theater closed in 1980 and fell into disrepair. In 1992, Richard and Hoa Brickley bought the theater and decided to turn it into the Fairbanks Ice Museum. The Ice Museum features four display cases that maintain a constant temperature of about twenty degrees. There, local artists display everything from a life-size moose or musk ox to a fish scene to full-size igloos, all made from ice. The museum used to feature a room where visitors could briefly feel a blast of winter in Fairbanks at twenty degrees below zero, but people didn't like to be that cold, according to the Brickleys. The Ice Museum is open only during the summer months and caters mainly to tourists. In the winter, the building is used as an inexpensive movie theater.

Rising continually from fire, Second Avenue was the heart of the Fairbanks commercial district almost from the beginning. However, it took until 1940, about the time this photo was taken, to pave any of the streets in Fairbanks, and Second Avenue was one of the first to be paved. Just right of center is the Empress Theater, which was built in 1927 by Austin E. "Cap" Lathrop. The

first Fairbanks building to be built entirely of reinforced concrete, the Empress was quite a sophisticated addition to the gold-rush town. It had 670 seats and brought top-shelf Hollywood films to the north. The theater shut down in the 1960s, in favor of gift shops in what's now called the Co-Op Building. The Mecca, to the right of the Empress, was one of Fairbanks' favorite bars.

In the pipeline boom years of the 1970s, Second Avenue had all but turned into one big tavern. To many, this was tolerable because of the money those establishments brought to the community as well as the constant street activity, which made people feel relatively safe. However, by the 1980s, after the pipeline was built and the price of oil plummeted, the area had emptied considerably and was considered blighted. The Fairbanks Development Authority got to work buying up liquor licenses and forcing many bars to move. The Mecca is now the only bar on the street, which mainly features cafés and gift shops. The Fairbanks Shakespeare Theatre Company has begun performing plays in the old Empress Theater, which is in the Co-Op Building, and the city continues to entice a younger breed of entrepreneurs to open up stores and help revitalize downtown Fairbanks.

In the early 1940s, when this picture was taken, Fairbanks had evolved from a scrappy gold-rush town into a major military outpost. From 1941 to 1945, the government spent $1 billion on Alaska defense and much of that was devoted to Fairbanks. This picture, taken on Second Avenue and Cushman, reflects the city's evolution: the streets are paved, and there's even a traffic light. Buildings of note in this picture include the Lacey Street Theater, which brought Hollywood to soldiers and citizens. The daily newspaper, the *Fairbanks Daily News-Miner*, had its offices next to the theater in the Lathrop Building. The Model Cafe, a Fairbanks institution since 1919, was one of the most popular restaurants in town. When President Warren Harding visited Fairbanks in 1923, he enjoyed a midnight banquet at the café. In 1940, heavyweight boxing champion Joe Louis visited Fairbanks, where he ate at the Model Cafe and watched a movie at the Lacey Street Theater.

The SpringHill Suites by Marriott now occupies a large part of First and Second avenues. Finished in 2001, the giant hotel displaced many small businesses, including what was once the Model Cafe, as well as many bars and liquor stores. However, the hotel has been a boon for downtown Fairbanks and is in keeping with Fairbanks' downtown revitalization program. Next to the SpringHill Suites is the Lathrop Building, which now houses the Lathrop Artists' Studios and a television station, among other businesses. On the corner is the Lacey Street Theater. The theater was—and still is—considered one of the finest pieces of architecture in Fairbanks and is currently home to the Fairbanks Ice Museum.

In the spring of 1903, the Northern Commercial Company bought a log trading post owned by E. T. Barnette, the founder of Fairbanks. The company immediately put up additions, including mercantile sales areas, storage, a power plant, a machine shop, and a telephone company, and dominated the Fairbanks riverfront. It has been said that the company built an empire. By 1907, the Northern Commercial Company grossed $2 million a year from this empire. To the west of the old Northern Commercial Company buildings is the Masonic Temple (second building from the right), which was purchased from the Tanana Commercial Company in 1908 and renovated for use as a club.

In the 1970s, Nordstrom opened a store on the spot where the Northern Commercial Company had been. It kept the peaked gable roof and some of the original windows of one of the structures. When Nordstrom announced plans to close the store in 1989, about 200 women protested outside the building. They did not prevail. Part of the original Northern Commercial Company's structure was still intact until 1992, when the last building was torn down to make way for a parking lot next to the Key Bank Building. Key Bank was completed in 1982, but traces its roots to 1905 and the Washington-Alaska Bank, the first one in Fairbanks. The bank was owned by E. T. Barnette, who had to leave town in the dead of night in 1911, after he was accused of swindling the bank's depositors.

After the gold that was easiest to get began to run out, the Fairbanks economy began to slump. However, by the 1930s, a new means to extract gold, called dredging, was in use. So, too, was the Alaska Railroad, which helped bring new prosperity to Fairbanks. This wooden city hall building on Cushman Street, which also housed a fire department, burned down in 1935. In the same year, it was replaced by the current building (shown opposite), which is considered an example of the modernized Classical Revival style. In 1933, President Franklin D. Roosevelt devalued the dollar and raised the price of gold to $35 an ounce, which ensured that Fairbanks remained immune to the ravages of the Great Depression, allowing for a relatively modern city hall building to be built.

The old city hall is now the Fairbanks Community Museum. Where the fire department used to be is now a series of small galleries in the former city offices, which display old photographs, maps, newspapers, and other bric-a-brac, as well as skillfully created explanatory exhibits, mostly focusing on the history and development of gold mining in the area. The Yukon Quest International Sled Dog Race shares these quarters, teaching about mushing with displays of equipment and raising funds for the race through the sale of souvenirs sold in the tiny gift shop. Plans are underway to turn Cushman, which is currently a one-way street, into a two-way street, and also to make it more pedestrian-friendly. City Hall is now where the "new" old Main School used to be, on Cushman Street.

The Alaska College Fairbanks

In 1915, Alaska's delegate to the U.S. Congress, James Wickersham, was successful in securing 250,000 acres of land for the Alaska Agricultural College and School of Mines. In 1917, the school was incorporated, and the first structure, the Main Building, was completed in 1918. However, due to the failure of the 1919 legislature to appropriate any funds for the college, it was boarded up and remained empty until 1922. On September 13, 1922, a large crowd gathered for the dedication ceremony. Soon, sixteen classes were offered to a student body of just six students. The early years were difficult, and the college was often on the verge of bankruptcy. In 1923, the first commencement produced one graduate, John Sexton Shanly. And so began the "Farthest North College," as it was called.

In the spring of 1960, the old Main Building was demolished to make room for other buildings. Pictured here is Bunnell Hall, which houses the Department of Journalism, the School of Management, and the Department of Biology and Wildlife; the offices of Space Planning and Management, Faculty Development, and Information Technology; as well as the Druska Carr Schaible Auditorium. The University of Alaska Fairbanks now has an enrollment of nearly 10,000. It's the only institution in the state that grants doctoral degrees, and home to seven major research units: the Agricultural and Forestry Experiment Station; the Geophysical Institute, which operates the Poker Flat Research Range; the International Arctic Research Center; the Arctic Region Supercomputing Center; the Institute of Arctic Biology; the Institute of Marine Science; and the Institute of Northern Engineering.

In the mid to late 1930s the center of campus at the Alaska Agricultural College and School of Mines was the center of scientific research in Alaska. The three-structure dormitory to the left is Hess Hall, the first permanent concrete dormitory on campus. The small house in the foreground was President Bunnell's home. Throughout Bunnell's twenty-seven years as president, he worked tirelessly, and his frugality led to a policy that most of the janitorial, food service, maintenance, and secretarial work was to be done by students working on a part-time basis. The students even built their own hockey rink, as well as the first three concrete buildings that make up the core of the campus. Beneath the smokestack is the two-story library and gymnasium, which is now called Signers' Hall.

On February 6, 1956, nearly 1,000 people witnessed the historic signing of the proposed Alaska constitution here. Because so many people showed up, the event was moved to the gymnasium, which is how it became known as Signers' Hall. Signers' Hall was completely renovated in 1984–85. The Elmer E. Rasmuson Library is right of center in this photo. It's named in honor of the president of the former Bank of Alaska. Rasmuson was also a member of the university's board of regents. The library opened its doors in 1970, and is now the state's largest library. It also holds pieces of art from some of Alaska's most well-known artists. The university remains an important center for scientific study in Alaska.

In 1903, the first district judge of the Alaska interior, James Wickersham, arrived in Fairbanks by dogsled, determined to lend Fairbanks legitimacy. He soon moved the seat of the Third Judicial Court to Fairbanks, which, because of the resulting government offices, ensured the survival of the town. He had several wooden courthouses built, all of which promptly burned down. In 1931, as a territorial congressman, he was finally able to secure funding for the building. The U.S. Post Office and Court House, which occupied one whole block in downtown Fairbanks, was designed in an Art Deco style from reinforced concrete. It was an imposing presence in a town still primarily composed of log structures. Wickersham was a lifelong booster for Alaska. He helped pass the bill granting Alaska territorial status, and he introduced the first bill to give Alaska statehood.

The building was used until 1977 to house various government agencies, including the U.S. District of Alaska, the U.S. Postal Service, the FBI, the EPA, and the U.S. Census Bureau. Although the building is now rented out for private office space, the building has changed little. Inside, it's still rich with decorative elements such as marble steps, brass-bordered terrazzo floors, verd antique marble panels above the front doors, and wrought-iron grillwork throughout. One by one, many of Fairbanks' historic buildings have disappeared over the years. Some were the victims of fires, some were torn down to make way for new developments, and others simply became too dilapidated to save. Today, Fairbanks has fewer than twenty-five properties listed on the National Register of Historic Places, including the Federal Building. Most of these historic buildings are owned by either local government agencies or for-profit businesses or organizations.

The Starting of The Great Fire In Fairbanks Alaska, May 22 nd

It was a hot, dry spring day on May 22, 1906, when a dentist used an alcohol light on his desk to heat his instruments. A breeze from an open window blew a curtain into the flame. From there, the fire spread throughout the city. Men dynamited buildings to try and contain the fire before it spread to the Northern Commercial Company's warehouses on First Avenue, which held much of the city's food supply. Legend has it that the warehouse was spared after the manager of the company ordered the store's bacon supply to be thrown into the broiler in order to build water pressure. An unofficial estimate placed the losses at about $1 million, and headlines promised a "New and Better Town Arising from Smoking Ruins."

In 1974, the Northern Commercial Company, the great economic engine of Fairbanks that had been doing business in the community since 1903, sold its stores in Fairbanks to Nordstrom, which shut down in 1989. Where the building used to stand is a parking lot, next to the Key Bank Building. That building was erected in 1982, but was once Fairbanks' first bank, owned by founder E. T. Barnette, and was, like much of Fairbanks, continually beset by fires. Before 1950, commercial buildings were often insulated with sawdust, a practice that is now disallowed by building codes. Buildings downtown are now made of concrete and steel, not green lumber that was cheap and abundant but subject to fires. A plan by community leaders and planners is in the works to revitalize the downtown area, including this stretch of First Avenue. The plan includes more shops and awnings, as well as pedestrian-friendly streets.

On July 22, 1902, Felix Pedro discovered gold on Pedro Creek, sixteen miles northeast of Fairbanks. Pedro's discovery launched a gold rush in the area that resulted in other discoveries and the establishment of camps in and around Fairbanks' waterways. Until the 1920s, numerous small mining companies and prospectors used crude underground mining methods to extract nearly $7 million worth of gold. By 1920, miners had exhausted the supply of readily accessible gold. Then, a subsidiary of the United States Smelting, Refining and Mining Company, the Fairbanks Exploration Company (the FE Co.), entered the scene. The FE Co. invested more than $10 million in equipment and construction for the operation of eight giant dredges. One of those eight dredges, dredge No. 8, seen here, was manufactured in 1927–28 by the Bethlehem Steel Company's Ship Building Division. The equipment was shipped from Pennsylvania by the transcontinental railroad and by ocean-going barge to the Alaskan Railroad to be assembled in early 1928.

Shut down in 1959, dredge No. 8 still stands about ten miles north of Fairbanks. The dredge has a forty-three-foot-high bow-gantry, which supported the belt-driven bucket line. The sixty-eight buckets could carry up to six cubic feet and 1,583 pounds. The bucket line discharged gravel through a screen with perforations of various sizes. During the process, an occasional large nugget would stick in the screens as the dredged material traveled the decline. Mostly, though, the relatively heavy gold fell through the screens and the rocks and gravel passed onto a conveyor belt and were discharged. Also, nozzles washed the gold from the gravel before it was carried to the tailing pile behind the dredge. This process resulted in the removal of approximately 97 percent of the gold from the rich gravel. The dredge and the surrounding area are now a National Historic District and a popular tourist attraction where one can pan for gold and have it weighed.

In 1904, Charles and Belle Hinckley started their dairy in downtown Fairbanks to serve a gold-rich town. In 1915, they moved the dairy to its current location between Farmer's Loop and College Road. In 1928, Charles and Anna Creamer bought the dairy and named it—quite appropriately—Creamer's Dairy. The dairy became modernized in the 1930s. To celebrate the new equipment, the Creamers held a party and invited the entire city of Fairbanks. The dairy thrived in the 1940s and 1950s, selling dairy products to the military. By the late 1950s, the Alaska Marine Highway and increasing air cargo gave rise to competition. By 1966, the dairy ceased producing dairy products.

After the dairy ceased production in 1966, the town of Fairbanks lobbied the state to buy the 1,800 acres of land and the buildings, which consisted of the family residence, visitor center, barn, processing building, and the bunkhouse and potato storage shed. The site is now the Creamer's Field Migratory Waterfowl Refuge, supervised by the Alaska Department of Fish and Game. Thousands of sandhill cranes, trumpeter swans, Canadian geese, ducks, and songbirds from as far away as South America descend on the refuge throughout the year. Trails throughout the acreage are used by mushers, skiers, skijorers, and amblers.

In the late nineteenth century, word of gold first brought prospectors to Ester Creek, about ten miles south of Fairbanks. By 1907, around the time of this photograph, Ester City had a population of about 200. The gold industry was thriving, and so was the town. It had a social hall, which was used for Sunday services, movies, card games, parties, and dancing. The town also had five saloons, a couple of hotels—one of which was called the Hotel California—and, of course, a grocery store. Eventually, gold production began to decline and so did the population. When the Fairbanks Exploration Company built a permanent camp for underground mining operations in the 1930s, Ester City had a population of three.

When the Fairbanks Exploration Company came to Ester City, it revitalized a dying town. However, it also brought large-scale open-pit mining, using floating dredges and draglines, and, in the process, removed much of the original town site, which is east of the town and overgrown with brush and trees. When most of the gold had been extracted by the 1950s, Ester began to remake itself as a tourist destination. What was once called the Cripple Creek Resort, and then the Ester Gold Camp, is a collection of Fairbanks Exploration Company buildings from the 1930s, which have been converted into a restaurant, hotel bar, and stage. During the summer months, tourists eat at the restaurant and then head to the Malemute Saloon, where locals put on a music variety show featuring Robert W. Service's poetry. The community of a few hundred or a few thousand, depending on where you draw the boundaries, is considered eccentric, even by Alaska standards. During a particularly contentious zoning meeting, a Fairbanks politician called Ester "the People's Republic of Ester." It's a name that has stuck, proudly.